POETRY MATTERS

Edited by Jenni Bannister

The UK

First published in Great Britain in 2011 by:
YoungWriters
Remus House
Coltsfoot Drive
Peterborough
PE2 9BF
Telephone: 01733 890066
Website: www.youngwriters.co.uk

Book Design by Samantha Wood

SB ISBN 978-0-85739-370-8

Foreword

Since our inception in 1991, Young Writers has endeavoured to promote poetry and creative writing within schools by running annual nationwide competitions. These competitions are designed to develop and nurture the burgeoning creativity of the next generation, and give them valuable confidence in their own abilities.

This regional anthology is one of the series produced by our latest secondary school competition, *Poetry Matters*. Using poetry as their tool, the young writers were given the opportunity to tell the world what matters to them. The authors of our favourite three poems were also given the chance to appear on the front cover of their region's collection.

Whilst skilfully conveying their opinions through poetry, the writers showcased in this collection have simultaneously managed to give poetry a breath of fresh air, brought it to life and made it relevant to them. Using a variety of themes and styles, our featured poets leave a lasting impression of their inner thoughts and feelings, making this anthology a rare insight into the next generation.

Contents

Vithushini Rajeswaran (16) 1

Beauchamps High School, Wickford

Kirstin Restarick (11) 1
Bronwen Paxton (11) 2
Thomas Kidd (11) 2
Daisy Palmer (11) 3
Jessica Olomofe (11) 3
Aaron Sinfield (11) 4
Sean Tupman (11) 4
Melissa King (11) 5
Alisha Eden (11) 5
Jasmine Thorne (11) 6
Sarah Moseley (17) 6
Hannah Jeffery (17) 7
David Fulton (17) 8
Jordan Simpson-Porter (17) 9
Riah Milne (17) 10
Anthony Parker (17) 11
Ela Broderick-Basar (17) 12

Brynmawr School, Brynmawr

Ashleigh Regan (12) 14
Hannah Hodges (12) 14
Emilia Guzzo (12) 15
Ryan Stoneman (12) 16
George Morgan (12) 16
Demi-Jay Leonard (12) 17
Kelly-Ann Sargeant (12) 17
Liam Cornock (13) 18
Chloe Bates (12) 18
Toby Thompson (12) 19
Rhys Bridgeman (13) 20
Rachel Evans (13) 20
Caitlin Sheppard (12) 21
Kieran Dobbs (13) 21
Angel Williams (12) 22
Abigail Jones (12) 22
Elise Baskerville (12) 23
Carrick Zerbino (12) 23
Connor Flook (12) 24
Tila-Dawn Edmunds (12) 25

Burlington Danes School, London

Salma Seidu (12) 25
Monet Bristol (12) 26
Amal Elouahabi (12) 27
Kion James (12) 27

Central Foundation School for Girls, London

Cherry Whipp (15) 28
Elizabeth Clayden (15) 30
Tamanna Rahman (14) 30
Nadia Aktar (14) 31
Aklima Begum (15) 31
Tashnim Siddique (13) 32
Amina Jama (13) 33
Samiha Hussain (15) 34
Sayidah Hussain (15) 35
Rahina Begum (15) 36
Fowzia Khan (18) 37

Connaught School for Girls, London

Charlotte Mulcahy (11) 38
Aisha Durrani (13) 39

Eastwood School, Eastwood

Lili-Anne Cooper (12) 40
Maddison Baldwin (11) 41
Millie Gallagher (11) 42
Georgina Hewlett-Moore (11) 43
Nicola Cocks (12) 43
Bradley Martin (11) 44

Callum Brady (12) 45

Harris School, Rugby

Katie Partridge (13) 46
Rhys Bradbury (14) 46
Hannah Coupland (14) 47
Thomas Ricketts (14) 48
Jack Finch (14) 48
Clare Drury (14) 49
James Was (13) 49
Adam Gould (12) 50
Andrew Love (13) 50
Robin Smith (13) 51
Stewart Ashton (13) 51
Reiss Boon (14) 52
Robert Scott (13) 52
Hannah Morgan (14) 53
Bronte Wrist (12) 53
Shay McNair (14) 54
Dominique Beards (13) 55
Joe Barnes (12) 56
Dan Malin (13) 56
Jessica Young (11) 57
Jade Smith (13) 57
Holly Burgess (14) 58
Mitchell Hughes (13) 58
Alana John (13) 59
Connor Mellet (12) 59
Himesh Parmar (12) 60
Aimee Martin (13) 60
Patrick Challen (11) 61
Jamie James (10) 61
Ellie Langhorn (12) 62
Troy Loveridge (11) 62
Jake Richardson (12) 63
Carolina Trincão (12) 63
Georgie Clark (14) 64
Nicky Tattal (13) 65
Ned Morley-Cottrell (11) 66
Sonny Hodder (11) 66
Tom Truslove (11) 67
Daniel Hood (11) 68
Beth Gillin (14) 69
Jack Wallace (11) 70

Highams Park School, London

Annah Butt (16) 70
Jennifer Pearl Johnson 71

Highcrest Community School, High Wycombe

Kaitlyn Festa (11) 72
Krislin Browne (12) 73
Sania Tahir (11) 73
Saira Azhar (11) 74
Katie Willoughby (11) 75
Adam O'Toole (11) 75
Jacob Creswick (11) 76
Rahima Islam (11) 77
Lamar Edwards (12) 78
Husna Malik (11) 80
Aleisha Starkey (11) 80
Matthew Snudden (12) 81
Adam Lipinski (11) 81
Toni Haywood (12) 82
Bienhaneen Hussain (11) 82
Charlotte Rumsey (11) 83

Liskeard School & Community College, Liskeard

Joe Andrews (11) 83

Mount Carmel RC Girls' School, London

Samrawit Russom (12) 84
Olivia Smith (12) 85
Toyin Olukosi (13) 86
Jade Mohamed (12) 86
Nkemjika Peace-be Ben-Nwankwo (11) 87
Khadija Khan (12) 88
Alezandra Stevens-Dyal (11) 89
Gemma Cooper (12) 90
Cansel Gok (12) 91
Milen Rosum (12) 92

Paige Cassidy (11).. 93
Georgia Wallace (13).. 94
Lara Gomes (13).. 95
Chanté Sylvester (13).. 96
Christiana Wynter (11).. 97
Emma Winful (11).. 98
Stephanie Odidika (12).. 99
Agatha Xavier (12).. 100
Shabnoor Ali (12).. 101
Zephania Osei-Bonsu (11).. 102
Adwaa Choudhury (11).. 103
Danielle Famiyesin (11).. 104
Lorissa Kaja (11).. 105
Megan-Alicia Jones (12).. 106
Maria Babalola (11).. 117
Ore Olukoga (12).. 118
Colette McNamara (11).. 119
Lauren Hopson (11).. 120
Mali Swift-Wilson (11).. 121
Tasnim Akter (12).. 122
Selena Siedlecka (12).. 122
Tiana Taleah Phyneasha James (11).. 123
Nahima Choudhury (11).. 123
Pelin Dogan (11).. 124
Glorianna Famuyiwa-Kennedy (11).. 126
Georgia Higgins (11).. 128
Wendy Fozoo (12).. 129
Joanna El Hajjar (12).. 130
Chloe Barrow (12).. 131
Chanda Chileshe (12).. 132
Mehret Zelalem (12).. 133
Chanelle Foskett (13).. 134
Lauren Stafford (12).. 135
Shannia Candice Carson (11).. 136
Hiremala Mesfun (11).. 136
Whitney Ikenwe (11).. 137
Natalie Kyereme (11).. 138
Megan Stuart (11).. 139
Louise Lau (12).. 140
Angelika Wroblewska (12).. 141
Shameika Precious Tello-Smith (13).. 142
Tasnim Chowdhury (11).. 143
Doyin Ajiboye (11).. 144
Lashai Modest-Norville (12).. 146
Ihuoma Anyanwu (11).. 147
Carina Abrue (11).. 148
Nada Alkhafaji (11).. 150

Paddington Academy, London
Zohra Dost Mohammad (13).. 151

Pontarddulais Comprehensive School, Swansea
Elliot Brace (12).. 152
Holly Archer (13).. 152
Molly Davies (12).. 153
Liam Oak (13).. 154

Robert Bloomfield Middle School, Shefford
Charlie Clarke (12).. 154
Sophie Tate (13).. 155
Kayleigh Jupp (12).. 156
Olivia Hitchen (13).. 156
Lauren Wylot (12).. 157
Katie Summerfield (13).. 158
Ryan Coxall (13).. 158
Ryan Donohoe (12).. 159
Emily Ashwin (12).. 159
Laura Warren (13).. 160
Charlotte Buckingham (13).. 160
Sophie Dear (11).. 161
Charlie Maxwell (11).. 161
Lucie Baker (12).. 162
Dionne Gray (13).. 164
Rachel Silverwood (12).. 165
Corrie Puleston (13).. 166
Cameron Mitchell (11).. 166
Finley Chapman (11).. 167
Bethany Kay (11).. 167
Ella Ofstedahl (13).. 168

Lucy Fredrickson (12) 168
Joshua Rayner (12) 169
Millie Ramsay Waite (11) 169
Kyah Rooney (13) 170
Ryan White (12) 171
Gregory Hill (12) 172
Adam Buckingham (12) 173
Harvey Lake (12) 174
James Hitchen (13) 175
Harvey Peirson (12) 176
Lewis McCracken (13) 177
Kelsey Newlin (11) 178
Leyla Ghaemi (11) 178
Amy Hannan (11) 179
Megan Sizer (11) 179
Brittany Mooney (11) 180
Max Potter (11) 181
Antonia Nannetti (11)
& Ellen Musgrove (12) 182
Georgia Pickett (11) 183
Jessica Badgery (11) 184
Zak Jest (11) 186
Madeline Symonds (12) 187
Holly Smith (11) 188
Amber Bailey (11) 189
Olivia Sandhu (11) 190
Cameron Burgess (11) 191
Jake Stanton (11) 192
Basmah Malik (12) 193
Rachel Hookway (11) 194

St Sampson's High School, Guernsey

Toby Falla (15) 195

Tarporley High School, Tarporley

Lucy O'Neill (12) 196

Tewkesbury School, Tewkesbury

Jack Bennetts (11) 196
Eleanor Gilbert (13) 197
Verity Briggs (12) 198
Kristina Bobs (12) 198
Emily Healey (13) 199
Ellie Hainsworth (13) 200
Bethan Skuse (14) 201
Jenna Roberts (13) 202

Walthamstow School For Girls, London

Enida Sadiku (11) 202
Amina Khanova (11) 203
Samintha Thavarajah (11) 203
Natalie Brady (11) 204
Namra Malik (12) 206
Salma Patel (11) 207
Lola Grieve (11) 208
Atiya Pervez (11) 210

Ysgol Gyfun Gymraeg Glantaf, Cardiff

Hannah Watkin (11) 210
Nia Phillips (11) 211
Tezni Bancroft-Plummer (11) 211
Amelia Smith (11) 212
Mared Edwards (12) 212
Llion Marc Carbis (11) 213
Emily Ogonovsky (11) 213
Sam Lipetz-Robic (17) 214
Rhodri Siôn Skyrme (11) 215
Caleb Roberts (11) 216
Holly McCormick (11) 216
Elin Nia Lewis (11) 217
Hannah Roberts
& Kirsty Louise French (11) 218
Mari Ann Bull (11) 219
Dafydd Manley (11) 220
Sioned Elin Rowlands (12) 221
Molly Turner (11) 222
Ashbei Holland (13) 223
Morgan-Leigh McCarthy (11) 224
Georgia Lewis (13) 225

The Poems

My True Red

Like the bronzing leaves winter ends its lonely freeze carrying the smell of blossoms in the breeze.
Like my dream I can feel the heat of summer in red's eyes and touch of winter in red's heart.
The river merges with sea, desires in our hearts merge with silence.
Like a lifeless tree on a winter's night, I stand as time goes by, I await for red's true reply.
Though I cannot have red my desires are like a blinding illumination,
Because an everyday red light shines brighter.
Red is real, red is love, red is confusion, red is forever, but will red be there for me whenever?

Vithushini Rajeswaran (16)

What Matters To You?

16 hands, chestnut brown,
Mane and tail hanging down,
Walking, trotting, canter too,
She's the horse that's right for you.
Her eyes will glow on cold, wet nights,
When the owls are awake and there's nothing to see
She will stare out her stable and hope to be free.
When you ride her she's steady and knows what to do,
But once you leave her, she will chase after you.
16 hands, chestnut brown,
Mane and tail hanging down,
Walking, trotting, canter too
She's the horse that's right for you.

Kirstin Restarick (11)
Beauchamps High School, Wickford

That's What Matters To Me

What matters to me is my family
And filling their faces with glee
What matters to me is my family
That's what matters to me.

What matters to me is swimming
I feel like I can be free
What matters to me is swimming
That's what matters to me.

What matters to me is my friends
And making sure they're not lonely
What matters to me is my friends
That's what matters to me.

Bronwen Paxton (11)
Beauchamps High School, Wickford

Facebook

F acebook is fun
A nd very cool
C onnect with people from around the world
E asy to log in, getting started
B rilliant games that you can play
O nline whilst on it you make new friends
O nce on it you can delete your account
K eep connected every day.

Thomas Kidd (11)
Beauchamps High School, Wickford

My Family

Family, family, they mean a lot to me
When I'm sad
They never make it bad
Give me love
Like the doves above.
I will never forget them.

Daisy Palmer (11)
Beauchamps High School, Wickford

Trapped!

I'm running so fast my paw is bleeding.
I'm leaping every step but I'm still speeding.
Then he comes with his trap ready
I'm walking still, still and steady.
Walk! Trip! Catch!
I think this is the end
Goodbye to my family,
Goodbye to my friends.

The man is now laughing and having fun,
I'm lying here trapped, my life is now done!

Jessica Olomofe (11)
Beauchamps High School, Wickford

Arsenal

Arsenal, Arsenal
The best team around
They play football at Emirates ground
Ven Persie, Fabregas, are the best
Every single match they play
Football, football, football
If you didn't kick the ball or even root around
It just would not be the same.

Aaron Sinfield (11)
Beauchamps High School, Wickford

My Dog Chewie

My dog Chewie is funny
He likes to chase bunnies
My dog's hobby is to poo and wee
He also likes to drink tea
He isn't the smartest dog around
But I am glad he was the one we found.

Sean Tupman (11)
Beauchamps High School, Wickford

What Dancing Feels Like

Feeling fresh
Feeling good
Feeling like I always should
Tapping my feet
Dancing to the beat
Nothing will change
It makes me feel free
It's just me!

Melissa King (11)
Beauchamps High School, Wickford

Always There For Me

F riends, friends will always be there for me
R unning around for you and me
I ndividuals but always together
E xciting days are always with you
N othing ever splits us up
D ead or alive we'll be together
S ide by side.

Alisha Eden (11)
Beauchamps High School, Wickford

What Matters To Me

What matters to me,
My one of a kind family,
My mum, dad, sister and me,
Everyone in my family.
But what also matters to me,
Is my friends who are always there for me,
Everyone matters to me.

Jasmine Thorne (11)
Beauchamps High School, Wickford

Only Child

The day you came was bittersweet,
A new toy and an enemy wrapped up in a blanket.
Every grown-up rushed to hear your siren,
Hushed mine.
Her time was divided now, not saved only for me and
The bedtime stories alone without you.

Possessive yells which drew all attention
That I was not ready to give up for you.
A planet orbited by admiring gazes,
Me, the moon.
The day you came was bittersweet,
Farewell the only child.

Sarah Moseley (17)
Beauchamps High School, Wickford

Untitled

I want red hair.
As red as the morning sun,
Rising on the hillside.
As dark as a drop of blood,
From your pricked thumb.
Red like a rose,
In its full blossom, yet –
The rose always dies.

I want brown hair.
As chestnut as a fallen conker.
Brown like the antique clock,
Gathering dust on the mantelpiece, yet –
Time could always stop.

I want blonde hair.
As blonde as the cornfields,
In the evening mist.
As fair as a feather from a young chick,
So fragile and delicate yet –
It could so easily break.

The roots are starting to grow back,
Each shoot symbolising that there is sign of life.
I feel them, so soft,
Like a newborn child's head of hair.
I'm being re-born, from my head to my toes,
I'm a woman again, free at last.

Hannah Jeffery (17)
Beauchamps High School, Wickford

Ashes, We Rise

For a second chance
What price do you pay?
A stand, a protest
That sees the light of day?

For whenever I have been doubted
Sat on, trampled over, slain.
An end result of positivity
Would ease the force of pain.

For everyone has a critic, an enemy
To ruin their views, their life.
But to disregard, to ignore,
Through the hate and strife.

For my love for defeating overwhelming odds
Makes me, you, everyone end the hurt.
For defying even the wildest dreamer
Kills the enemy, the doubt. Become introvert.

So for witnessing the destruction
The demolition of enemies, the demise.
You have joined an elite, from the dead,
To the ashes, we rise.

David Fulton (17)
Beauchamps High School, Wickford

The Kid

We came through the storm, nooses on our necks,
Locked in a box, without the combination for rights,
Kind of like the kid's previous situation,
300 years on . . . still shackled!
        A boy from the heart of the kingdom.

Thoughts of life out the ghetto . . . seemed wrong,
Who knows where the kid would be without a saviour,
With the thugs, knives, a gun?
        But he was staring down, another kind of barrel – failure!

He traded it all in to the countryside just to get his shine on,
The move ultimately switched his fate,
Now comes the shine, the chance to illuminate.
A kid just trying to do the opposite of left,
        As long as there is the opposite of death.

Moved out quite far,
But the furthest he went was out of his mind,
You get judged, you get looked at wrong,
        The struggle with being you.

The kid out of his zone, he can't go back to,
It's hard to turn on the hood that made you,
The tales of young black male,
Life that originally built to fail,
        But change gone come, change gone come.

From having 'dreams' to we 'cans'
In less than 47, now in Heaven
As the people who strived for us met there X,
        The kid reflects on the life he now leads.

Jordan Simpson-Porter (17)
Beauchamps High School, Wickford

Nature's Rubies

Crystals of morning dew
Rubies against blood red.
The priceless beauty
That is the red rose.

The roses grow
Untamed and unruly.
Soft, scarlet and free
Bloody and wild.

These treasures thrive
As nature intended.

Numb to their thorns
They feel no pain,
The roses grow
With their bodies entwined.

Blind to the sting
They stand embracing,
Dead to the thorns tearing
But none will weep.

For like love itself
Even the most beautiful things can hurt.

Riah Milne (17)
Beauchamps High School, Wickford

A Poem About Insomnia

Darkness but I can't sleep.
I lay there for hours, tossing and turning.
Thinking for hours just tossing and turning
So much on my mind I just can't sleep.

Crazy thoughts come and go
Dispersing themselves into the darkness
One by one they leave my brain only to be replaced
By crazy thoughts that come and go.

Restless as a baby.
You will try so hard but Satan has his grip.
The Devil will win and you will not sleep,
Restless as a baby.

You wonder why, try to find a reason
Searching your brains. The library of information.
It must be there somewhere, a simple solution
You wonder why, try to find a reason.

Unimaginable ideas throughout your body.
Some good, some bad, some entirely indifferent.
Some are black, some are white, others colourless.
Just unimaginable ideas throughout your body.

You go to bed late hoping
Tiredness will help. Still you lay there
Watching the clock. *Tick-tock, tick-tock*,
You go to bed late hoping
The rooster crows at 6.30am
You're up to make him breakfast
You've been up for hours
6.30am doesn't seem early.

There must be a solution to this
Something someone can do.
In reality - that would be too good
To be true.

Anthony Parker (17)
Beauchamps High School, Wickford

The Poem

Writing this poem has taught me something:
I am no good at writing poems.
My many thoughts whizz around my head
And they're too hard to catch. I'm scared.
Scared you will not want to hear my work,
Oh the topic! War, love, starving donkeys!
And my head cries but I don't do meaningful!
Oh crikey.

Have you ever tried to write a poem
On reality TV? I did.
'This is Big Brother.' And
'Who is she?' 'Where did you find her?'
'Keeping up with the Kardashians'
And 'The Simple Life'
I am a reality TV junkie.
Scrap that.

The topic of superheroes?
A worthwhile topic, at last!
It seems to me this world needs
A saviour, a superhero!
Saving from the real-life
Diabolical villains
But what, is a hero's essence,
Who is a hero in your eyes?
I wish I had a cape.
Perhaps not.

The topic of my mother
Surely it's easy to write about
Someone you love, like your mum!
You see, my mother is one
Funny lady. A complete oddity.
I could say she's like a Snickers
But there's nothing remotely
Chocolatey about her 'cept
She's rather nutty like me!
Oh dear.

Maybe my mother's cooking
Will stir some emotive language!
I really don't enjoy my mum's cooking
Which I know is excessively rude!
Can I help that I do not relish watery pasta
Meat or mayo upon my food?
Oh no.

A poem is a hard task,
A task of shaping words.
You may not laugh or cry
But you saw and delved into
My little crazy brain!
And basically you just wasted
Your time reading a poem about
A poem. Ha-ha . . . ha!

Ela Broderick-Basar (17)
Beauchamps High School, Wickford

Best Friends

My best friends make me happy, they believe in me.
Every moment is spent together, stupid, funny, angry moments.
They are trustworthy and take control when I can't.
They remember my favourite things and are always happy for me.
They are always there for me but still depend on me.
Best friends are special, don't take them for granted!

Ashleigh Regan (12)
Brynmawr School, Brynmawr

Family

You only ever have one family
Someone out there would love to have yours
Mistake after mistake they're always there
To back you up because they care.

So never forget you've got them
Cherish them every day
Tell them you love them
And don't push them away.

Hannah Hodges (12)
Brynmawr School, Brynmawr

Bullying

'What's going on?'
'I'm being picked on.'
'Who would do that to you? You're new.'
'I think that's the reason they're being so harsh.'
'So why don't you tell me right from the start?'
'I don't know what to say or even where to begin,
I feel my life is ending when it should be starting to begin.'

'What's going on?'
'Silly notes passed around,
Dirty looks on the playground
They're making me feel like I don't belong
They're making me feel
Scared,
Upset,
Alone.'

'What's going on?'
'It's all going to change,
I've told!
I've told someone what's going on.
She understands, she knows they've done wrong.'
'That's great so do you feel better inside?'
'Yes, it's all over, I'm happy now,
Not sad, not anymore.'

Emilia Guzzo (12)
Brynmawr School, Brynmawr

Fifa!

F ootball is amazing
I nter Milan are a good football team
F air even if you're bad you should be treated the same
A wesome goals.

Fifa is a supporting game
People walk in fame, some in shame.

This is my message to all of you
Treat everyone the same.

Ryan Stoneman (12)
Brynmawr School, Brynmawr

Holiday Heaven

I go on holiday on a plane,
I look in the brochure and look at Spain.
Landing is the worst
Your ears always burst!
Looking out of the window at the clouds
All I can hear are the loud sounds.

In the pool it is so cool
You know all the other kids drool.
The diving boards are fun
And it really hurts your bum
And everyone thinks you're dumb.

George Morgan (12)
Brynmawr School, Brynmawr

Home

Home is when you feel loved.
Home is when your family are around.
Home is when the fire is on.
Home is when you listen to the rain outside.
Home is when you're all cuddled up on the sofa with your PJs on.
Home is when your family listen to your problems and understand you.
Not many people have homes or family, never be ungrateful!

Demi-Jay Leonard (12)
Brynmawr School, Brynmawr

Friends

Friends are not always there for you.
Respect is important to your friends.
If they bully you tell someone.
Life is for living, not for bullying.
Everyone you know is not always your friend.
Stand up for yourself, don't let them bully you.
Never let them get you down,
Don't take any messing from them.
Let's sort it out and stop it.
So this is a message for you,
Bullies are not nice.

Kelly-Ann Sargeant (12)
Brynmawr School, Brynmawr

Running, I'm Running

I'm running, I'm running
So very fast
And I'm moving my arms and legs
Back and forth, back and forth.

I'm running, I'm running
Across the field
Thinking, can I overtake?
And where to go next.

I'm running, I'm running
I think to myself, how good would it be
If I won and got all the glory?
I start to feel success around me.

Getting tired but I can't slow down
I win the race
No need to frown.

Liam Cornock (13)
Brynmawr School, Brynmawr

Drama

D rama is my big ambition, hope and dream
R ecords repeating going round and round is like me and singing
A cting is when my mind goes miles away
M y mum ends up roaring up the stairs for me to shut up
A bright shining sun is like my face when I'm performing.

Chloe Bates (12)
Brynmawr School, Brynmawr

Call Of Duty

COD oh COD,
I'm on my tod,
In my room,
And suddenly . . . *boom!*

I shoot, I shoot,
I reload and shoot.
Sadly I'm gone.
Then the voiceover comes on.

I get up, keep calm and carry on.
The screen comes back,
Dark and black.
I gain my strength, but still out of breath.

I go down on one knee,
With a blood pool beside me.
I'm angry and fierce,
And crying with tears.

I complete the level and achieve a medal,
But soldiers out there,
Do not play,
They focus and concentrate,
It's not a game they play.

Toby Thompson (12)
Brynmawr School, Brynmawr

Cardiff City!

This is a message to the fans, do not fight or else you're banned.
Craig Bellamy going down the wing
What you going to do? Sing, sing, sing
We are top of the league; we are top of the league
We got the king of the wing,
What's his name?
Chris Burke.

Rhys Bridgeman (13)
Brynmawr School, Brynmawr

Bullying

Bullying, bullying is not nice
Stop it now before someone loses their heart and soul.
Punching, kicking and pushing, it is all bullying.
Bullying is bad, bullying is mean
Bullying is painful to the person you're doing it to.
Stop it now before you lose your friends and family.

Rachel Evans (13)
Brynmawr School, Brynmawr

Friendship

Friends are very important in your life.
They help you thorough the rough times,
They do things with you.
Never give up on trying to please,
They put you on the right track.
Remember your memories, they're with you on everything.
Excited for each other, we have sleepovers in the holidays.
We're together in all of your situations.

Caitlin Sheppard (12)
Brynmawr School, Brynmawr

Cars

C ars are small, cars are large, cars are fast, cars are slow
A lloys on wheels, coloured and shiny, alloys are big and small too
R adios and stereos make us mad but I guarantee you that they won't
make us sad
S peed matters for people, speed is worrying for people too

So please guys listen to signposts or otherwise you will kill someone!

Kieran Dobbs (13)
Brynmawr School, Brynmawr

My Family Loves Me!

M y family's fab because they love me
Y ou're not lucky like me because of love

F amily is as free as can be
A ll day, day in, day out
M um is cool because she ain't no fool
I love my family and they love me
L oving family cares for a good day
Y ou're all mine and I ain't got to pay

L ove makes the world go round
O ur family has ups and downs
V ery, very good to me
E veryone deserves a family like mine
S ome say I wish I had a family like that

M y family's fab because they love me
E veryone should be more like me.

Angel Williams (12)
Brynmawr School, Brynmawr

What Matters To Me

P erforming is what I love
E ach time I perform my heart beats like a drum
R ehearsing each time to get the lines right
F un as it may be everyone wants to succeed
O n the stage you forget who you are
R emembering the words you need to say
M agic it feels like when you're up there
A pplause from the audience is lovely to hear
N ervous feelings rush through you like butterflies
C urtains close applause still ringing in your ears
E xcitement in the air as the crowd ask for more.

Abigail Jones (12)
Brynmawr School, Brynmawr

My Family

My dad
Is not so bad

My step-mum
Has a big bum!

My grandma
Always says ta.

My grandpa
Goes too far
In his car.

My real mum
Is lots of fun!

My best friend
Will be my friend
Until the end!

Elise Baskerville (12)
Brynmawr School, Brynmawr

Nature

Nature is beautiful
Nature is wonderful
Busy buzzing bumblebees
Fly around the tall green trees

Butterflies flutter around the flowers
Busy fluttering for hours and hours
Stingy nettles sting
Happy bluebirds sing
Helpful hedgehogs help to move
Leaves that fall off our hedge.

Carrick Zerbino (12)
Brynmawr School, Brynmawr

Call Of Duty

COD oh COD
How I love my clan, oh my God
Feels so good when I kill that man
But he is good and kills the rest of my clan.
I am the last alive
But they still have five.
I see the one
And *boom*, he's gone.
Now there's only four
Camping by the back door.
I see two and they are gone
And now it is two versus one.
The bomb has been planted
And I get there quick,
He throws a stun
So I change my gun.
Boom! Headshot and he is gone
But I must hurry because they still have one.
But I can't see him anywhere
So I change my gun.
There he is behind the tree!
Would you believe I killed all three!
We win the game
And I defuse the bomb.
'This is great,' says my friend Tom.
I'm doing this just to improve my score,
Thank God I don't do it like others in a real war!

Connor Flook (12)
Brynmawr School, Brynmawr

Poverty!

Every time I turn on the television
I always have to look and listen.
The people living in poverty
Children and their families.
I show sympathy when they are going through it
And then I think, *what if it happened to me?*
How could I go through it?
I couldn't face it!
I see the sad expression upon their faces
As they don't go many places.
They make our clothes and don't get any credit.
That is why we try to solve it.
They get water from the rivers,
We moan and groan about little shivers.
We don't appreciate a lot,
They appreciate everything they have got!

Tila-Dawn Edmunds (12)
Brynmawr School, Brynmawr

Home

Home for me means where I can calm down and relax and where I can get my privacy.
Home is where I can call, 'Home, sweet home,' and where I feel safe and where I grew up.
Sometimes I quickly run home just to check if my house is still there
'Cause if I didn't have a house I wouldn't feel safe, like the way I am now.
'Cause there's no place like home.

Salma Seidu (12)
Burlington Danes School, London

Home

There's a room in my house where nobody goes except me,
It's a nice room, a safe room,
A where I go to relax room,
Any day or night room,
A free room.

There's a room in my house where nobody goes except me,
It's a cosy room, a bright room,
A where I go to watch TV room.

There's a room in my house where nobody goes except me,
It's a wonderful room, safe room,
A where I go sleep room.

There's a room in my house where nobody goes except me,
It's a quiet room, a blue room
A where I go to eat room,
Anytime, middle of the dark room,
A free room.

There's a room in my house where nobody goes except me,
A goal room, a private room,
A where I go play room,
That's all you have to know about me.

Monet Bristol (12)
Burlington Danes School, London

Home

Home is protective against the others.
Home is full of sisters and brothers.
Home is where you find your rest.
Home is where you feel the best.
Hold the glow in your eye,
Home is the emotion that makes you cry.
We meet wonderful things in our home
So make the peace one day.

Amal Elouahabi (12)
Burlington Danes School, London

Lightning Friend

The noise in the sky is
Angry and I know why
Because the lights are
Flickering and
Fighting nearby.

The thunder is awakening from
His sleep because the lights are
Bright and
Full of beauty tonight.
The sky is dark, darker then the moon
It shines as silver, as silver as a spoon.

The wave of colours that light up the sky
It's getting darker and saying goodbye.

Kion James (12)
Burlington Danes School, London

Lousy Reputation

Today he tastes of apple juice,
Old apple juice.
There is always someone like him
To cut out and fail.

And then the department store stench,
Sad enthusiasm. Don't forget to act surprised.
And I can smell you through your dress,
Hidden denim shrubbery.
Textbook terror.

What have you done to make him happy to see you?
Arm around you,
The bottom falling out of everything.
I am so jealous, so much that my
Perfume turns septic as ear infection medicine.
Unlovable.

What is in your bag?
Is it a voice box? Dye?
It smells like chloroform and looks like love.
O perfect cyst,
Marble female nude;
By the time you leave him he will be a taxidermy experiment.

How can you be so ungrateful?
He is a future, orange and in vampire make-up.
A private kind of happiness.

And you are relentless,
Soft steam train, trying to hurt everything.
Horrible.
I am just a child.
I don't mean to hurt anyone but myself.
Little statue,
So scared of you and stuck to the chair in dread.

It won't be long until you have a baby.

O, it was stretched death,
It was thumbscrews watching you two.
Hand in claw,
Hand on shoulder.
'What are you doing here?' and
Die on the escalator.

Cherry Whipp (15)
Central Foundation School for Girls, London

The Darkness

The heart is such a precious thing,
The world is so full of sin,
As your blood runs cold,
And drains from your skin.

The darkness quickly closes in,
The terror starts to begin,
As the world is swallowed,
There is no din.

Elizabeth Clayden (15)
Central Foundation School for Girls, London

My Love For You

Every step I take,
Every move I make,
I'll always think of you.

Every time I cry,
Every time I try,
I'll never forget you.

Every time I sing,
Every time my phone rings,
All I think about is you.

Every day as the roses beam,
Every day I'll always have a dream,
Having a sight of nothing but you.

Whether it's day or night,
Whether it's dark or light,
I know I'll always have you at every sight.

Tamanna Rahman (14)
Central Foundation School for Girls, London

Mother

Someone who stays awake for you,
Cries for only you,
Tries to fight every battle
Until she understands:
It is over.

Someone who watches out for you,
Cooks for you,
Cleans after you,
Sleeps after you.

Someone who shouts at you
But only for the right reason.
Someone who we take for granted.
Only a mother.

Nadia Aktar (14)
Central Foundation School for Girls, London

Thoughts

We always have thoughts in our mind
That are waiting to be read out.
People will be waiting to be inspired
By the thoughts of what you have in mind.

Some thoughts are really close to your mind
Whereas others may be mind blowing.
However, some thoughts may be personal
They are all inspirational for you to see.

There are thoughts that can bring back bad memories
Although the thoughts may be depressing but you can't go back.
So the thoughts will be staying to refresh your mind all the way
Through your journey of special adventure to make you a different person.

Aklima Begum (15)
Central Foundation School for Girls, London

What Is Important To Me?

The people I meet,
The food I eat,
The familiar faces
Or those special places.

My first foolish crush,
The one who made me blush.
Those memories of being a child,
Leather jackets, polka dots, 90s style!

My family, those whom I love
Sticking by me when push came to shove.
The laughter I shared
Lessons learnt through endless tears.

Or how about things that really matter?
People dying, starvation, the pain, the suffer.
Global warming, pollution, recession,
All these worries turning into obsession.

So what is important to me?
I'd have to dig deeper and see.
Maybe I'll figure it out
Next time my pen meets paper.

Tashnim Siddique (13)
Central Foundation School for Girls, London

Daddy's Little Girl

I'm Daddy's little girl, I know,
When we see each other our faces glow.
Just the thought of him in pain makes me cry
And I'll never handle it when he finally does die.

You see, Dad has suffered from Alzheimer's from when I was nine,
It developed too much and he'll never be fine.
When it first came about all I could do was shout
Though it always made my mum cry, more than usual,
And believe me, the feeling was mutual.

Crying a river would be easy,
Facing my dad, I started to feel queasy.
So I decide to avoid him completely
There's never a way to do that discreetly.

Instead I searched for someone to blame
But I never know, my siblings probably feel the same.
We never share a word
And I think that's what we all preferred.

So four years have passed,
I can't say it's been a blast.
I spent every day thinking that was his last
And all of a sudden, it went so fast.
I never found that someone to blame
But I guess that was never my aim.

I felt like Daddy's girl again today
And I said to myself, 'Hey, it never went away!'
I forever will be Daddy's girl I know,
Doesn't matter how much I grow.

Amina Jama (13)
Central Foundation School for Girls, London

I Remember Thou Smile

(In memory of my loving Grandfather)

I remember your smile, still images a picture in my mind,
While talking and thinking about you I have tears in my eyes.

I remember your eyes, bold and black they find a way to melt our hearts.
The line you used to say over and over again still continues throughout the generation.
The line itself makes me laugh just thinking about it,
Even though you're not here anymore you'll always be kept in our hearts.

I know none of us can stay, but you will always be so special to me.
In this Dunya (world) you will always live as a token of happiness and joy from God.
You were so strong and built, you carried me and my sister in one hand,
And then let us go again because we were tickly.
Also listening to stories of your adventurous childhood,
Oh how much you used to make us laugh!

Those sweets you used to bring us they were as sweet as a red strawberry.

Also you had your own way of doing stuff, who can forget your PFC,
Eating that just smashed everyone else's, but
Most of all I remember thou smile.

Samiha Hussain (15)
Central Foundation School for Girls, London

Twins

Twins, what's the first word that comes to your mind?
Friends, love and a joy to have
Well, not in our case, actually, not in our mum's case
She wanted us but didn't know what trouble we were going to be.

We're not like any other twins
We argue, never see eye to eye and we're the complete opposite.
People say twins are the best,
However, I go east and she goes west.

Everywhere we go we get the fame,
Some say we look different
Others say we look the same.
But we find it lame
Like experiencing the same déjà vu
Also like listening to a chorus from a song.

The differences between us have made the distance long
Only for a short period
But this, for the future
I know for sure
Will be a reason for getting more closer.

Our whole life we thought we're not identical
At the age of fourteen we finally find out
We have 97% chance of being identical
We try to hide the small disappointment as we lied.

As years go past we have our laughter and our cries
We'll never forget the lows and highs
We have had in our life.

Sayidah Hussain (15)
Central Foundation School for Girls, London

Without You!

I love you with all that's left in my heart
Without you
There will be no reason for me to shine
There will be no reason for me to breathe
Every breath
Without you
The world is colourless
And
My heart is an empty place
Without you
I can't live
I can't breathe
I can't sleep
I need you here with me right by my side
And
I want you to stay in my heart forever and make me shine.

Rahina Begum (15)
Central Foundation School for Girls, London

Grandad

When we were little we used to run around screaming -
You used to tell us to hush up.
When I couldn't read a book
You'd sit me on your lap and read me the story.
Usually I'd be the last one to finish my dinner
And unlike everyone else, you didn't tell me off.
But now you've softened up and I've grown up
You don't shout at me but do to the younger ones.
I sit next to you but you don't read stories to me anymore.
I don't run around screaming now
And I'm not the last one sat at the dinner table.
Instead you enjoy my company as I do yours
And love it when you smile cos under those wrinkles your heart is still beating
And the memories of you we want to add to
And like me these little ones will grow up and hope that you won't leave us
But be here to share all our achievements.

Fowzia Khan (18)
Central Foundation School for Girls, London

I Would Love To . . .

I would love to taste
The earth in which we stand
The grass in which we sit
The wild tangled greenery
The rough broken ground

I would love to smell
The warmness of your heart
Its thumping electricity
Its friendly beating
Wafting out towards me.

I would like to touch
Every word that you speak
I would put my hands to your lips
Feel the soft words you say
Slipping through my fingers.

I would like to see
Every breath that you take
The humming of your throat
The air inhaled and exhaled
In front of me.

I would like to see
The warmness of your smile
Every grin, every beam
The shine creeping out
Making us all happy.

Charlotte Mulcahy (11)
Connaught School for Girls, London

Best Friends For Life

(Dedicated to my best friend who lives elsewhere now)

When we were in Year 7, we were only eleven
Now look at us, we have grown our trust
I can't believe we're thirteen now, don't ask me how
We had a great time together and those memories will always last forever
You make me feel good like a real friend should
You were more than a friend to me and may this always be.

Then when the pain struck I felt like I was losing luck
When you told me you were leaving, I was having a hard time believing
That you were going to go so far away and didn't want to delay
So hard did I try, in front of you not to cry
But I guess it never worked, I thought my heart could never get cured
Cos you were the only person I could rely on but it's okay, you don't have to hear more.

I really miss you and I hope you miss me too
I hope you're having a great time, cos life here is as sour as lime
Time for me to say goodbye and goodnight
So here it goes, 'Stah u murra muzza bimbo!'

Aisha Durrani (13)
Connaught School for Girls, London

When I Become

When I become a teacher, of art, maths or PE
Yes, when I become a teacher I think I'll be
A fun loving teacher, that's what I'll be
And everyone will think, when they think of me
That teacher, she's cool, that teacher she's got edge
That teacher she's not boring, like books or veg
Yes, that's what I'll be, a teacher that dares
To play a few tricks, but still deeply cares.

Or maybe I'll be, a moany teacher
A boring, shouty, groany teacher
And people will think, when they see me slump by
Yawn, she's boring, and then look up at the sky
And say, she should just lighten up, it's light up there
I bet if she just smiled, she'd be lighter than air.

Oh no! Now I'm thinking, I don't know which one to choose
Should I be great and fun loving? Or a bit of a snooze?

Lili-Anne Cooper (12)
Eastwood School, Eastwood

Poetry Matters!

My friends and family,
My mum and dad,
My brother and sister,
They're all just fab.

When I am down
They're there for me.
There are also other reasons
Why I love them dearly.

Giggle, giggle, scream, scream,
We all have our moments
But in the end
We make a great team.

This is what matters a lot to me
My friends and my family
Loving and caring for me that's their job
And that is why I love them a lot!

Maddison Baldwin (11)
Eastwood School, Eastwood

What Would I Do Without?

They've been with me through everything
I've never had a doubt
They mean the world to me
I couldn't bear to be without

From days that I'm sad
To days when I'm so glad
To have such precious things close to my heart
Even when I'm . . .
Doing my hair or . . .
My mum making us share
Oh what would I do without.

Playschool to primary school to high school right now
Although they can't be with me
I feel that they are still here
Watching over me like a guardian angel
Every minute of every day
I hear them say
'Don't worry, you'll be okay'
Or when I'm hurt, upset or sad
They make me glad to have them right beside me
I don't know what I'd do without.

In a flash . . . *boom!*
Something's changed . . .
Something's missing . . .
Where did they go? . . .
Where's my best friend? . . .
A part of me has disappeared
My heart is broken
Collecting pieces of my life from the floor
The cold, grey floor
Now I know what I'd do without
The feeling has affected me in so many ways
Now I know what I'd do without!

Millie Gallagher (11)
Eastwood School, Eastwood

Holidays

H ot to trot
O range sand
L iving the sweet life
I nvigorating
D aydreams
A mazing abroad
Y ellow sun gold penny
S quawking seagulls.

Georgina Hewlett-Moore (11)
Eastwood School, Eastwood

Puzzle

My life is like a puzzle, every piece fits
But I am not sure where they go,
I find a new piece of the game every day,
In some ways, the puzzle is coming together
Now each piece is beginning to form day after day,
I lose pieces or I forget them,
Half of the puzzle is complete,
I still have a long way to go,
I know some day I will find that very last piece.

Nicola Cocks (12)
Eastwood School, Eastwood

What Matters To Me

I'll tell you what matters to me
All my friends and family.
My mum, my dad, my sister, my dog
My uncle, my auntie, my brother and COD.
My mum cares for me when I am sick
But she knows when I'm pulling a trick.
My dad lets me get away with some things
But I can't get past not doing the bins.
My sister is a douche sometimes
But I know she loves me and she knows I can rhyme.
My dog is a bull mastiff and he's cool
But he used to always fall in the pool.
My cousins can be funny a lot
But sometimes they're mad and lose the plot!

Bradley Martin (11)
Eastwood School, Eastwood

What Matters To Me?

What matters to me?
Is it a green tree?

What matters to me?
Sailing down the River Lee.

What matters to me?
Is it my family?

What matters to me?
Is it my PS3?

What matters to me?
Is it kicking a ball?

What matters to me?
Is it being cool?

What matters to me?
Is it anything at all?

Callum Brady (12)
Eastwood School, Eastwood

The Snow Leopard

She stalks across the cold snow,
Waiting for prey which did not know.

The elegant paws pressed onto the rocks,
Secret and cunning, like a fox.

She's always camouflaged from head to tail,
Her prey cannot escape as she does not fail.

She pounces with her sharpened claws,
Through the misty, white air in the sky she soared.

The sudden whistle of a bullet passed the air,
To smile on the shooter's face showed he didn't care.

The carcass got dragged away to be put into the van,
The men smiled of the success of their evil plan.

Two cubs lay under a tree watching their mother,
They buried their faces within each other.

Endangered animals are what matter to me,
I hope in the future the animals you will see.

Katie Partridge (13)
Harris School, Rugby

Family

Family love you, family care,
With them you're happy 'cause they're always there.
When you are with them, they fill you with joy,
Like when you were younger and got a new toy.
Without my family, what would I do?
Probably cry, wouldn't you?
My sisters, my nan, my mum and my dad,
Without them all, I'd be very sad.

Rhys Bradbury (14)
Harris School, Rugby

What's Important To Me?

My family and friends are what are important to me,
If I didn't have them then what would there be?
I need them there when things are tough,
They help me see that not everything is rough.

My family and friends are what are important to me,
If I didn't have them then what would there be?
They show me that not all things are bad,
Make me happy when I'm feeling sad.

My family and friends are what are important to me,
If I didn't have them what would there be?
They give me advice and show that they care,
I'm happy to know that they'll always be there.

My family and friends are what are important to me,
If I didn't have them what would there be?
They are the people who I most treasure
They help me through every single endeavour.

My family and friends are what are important to me,
If I didn't have them what would there be?
These are the people who always make me smile
They make my life all worthwhile.

My family and friends are what are important to me,
If I didn't have them what would there be?
The answer to that is nothing at all,
If I didn't have them then I would fall.

Hannah Coupland (14)
Harris School, Rugby

Family Matters

Spending time with your family,
Is what should matter most,
Enjoying brilliant holidays,
Together eating a Sunday roast.

Thanking the people that have raised you,
Reminiscing about the memories you've shared,
Laughing about the jokes,
And grateful for the future they've prepared.

Appreciating what they give,
Loving all the things they do,
Family matters most to me,
And so it should, to you.

Thomas Ricketts (14)
Harris School, Rugby

What Is Important To Me

Many things are important to me:
Friends will always be important to me
As long as they are with me to the end.
My name is important to me,
I don't care if it's lame.
My home is important to me because it keeps me safe
My family will always be important to me.
My dogs are important to me; they comfort me when I'm sad.
Coventry City is important to me because it's the family team.

Jack Finch (14)
Harris School, Rugby

What Matters To Me

When you speak to me, I listen.
When you guide me, I obey.

When I sing, I rejoice.
When I'm in need, I pray.

When you call me, I answer.
When you ask, I do.

When I need help, you are there
For everything I say and do.

When I am sorry, you forgive.
I know I'll always follow you.

Clare Drury (14)
Harris School, Rugby

Home

Home is where your soul is,
Life's mixed with depression of the overshadowing future,
From the lonely spider to the sleeping human,
The heart is where your home is.

Family relatives inspired by the past of the ever growing family tree,
Warmth, love and dreams protect against the icy fingers of the
Jack Frost spirit.
Forgiveness and inspiration entwine to create the place of rest
And tender love.

Home is where you sleep into the future.

James Was (13)
Harris School, Rugby

October

I could hear the sounds in the distance of the harvester cutting the corn,
The steam flowing swiftly through the valley in the dawn.
The beautiful October sunshine was streaming through the window.
What a lovely morning in the town of Lindow.
I walked through the swaying trees then I found lots of pennies,
I shouted 'Get in there my son.' Then I said to myself, 'Bum bum.'

Adam Gould (12)
Harris School, Rugby

What Matters To You?

What matters to me is my family, they are always there when I'm in trouble.
My friends help me when I'm stuck with something,
Even when I'm sad they are there to make me smile.
My education, to help me get a good job and life when I'm older.
My future so that I will do well when I'm older.
My home, it keeps me safe and secure and warm in the winter,
It relaxes me when I'm angry or sad, but most of all it keeps me happy!
My Xbox, to entertain myself when bored in my home, and to keep me happy as well.
My computer, so I can research on it how I want and when I want.
My bike, to help exercise me and to get somewhere easily.
My TV, to let me watch what I want when I want
And finally my phone, to let me keep in touch with mates and listen to music.

Andrew Love (13)
Harris School, Rugby

What Matters To Me

What matters to me is that I always have someone there.
What matters to me is that I have someone to care.
I need someone who will look out for me.
I need someone who will always be there for me.

What matters to me is that my three dogs are always happy.
What matters to me is that my family are always well.
I want them all to be happy
I want them to always feel great.

What matters to me is that I am treated fairly.
What matters to me is that I am shown respect.
I need to know that I'm understood.
I need to know that people understand what I feel.

Robin Smith (13)
Harris School, Rugby

A Dream

You told me in a dream you always loved me
I wept with joy at what with joy you said.
My sadness was not there. It was so lovely
And with you was my darling, also dead.
The sky was with an early sunrise burning,
Yet still with ample darkness for the moon,
Which held the secret of its youthful yearning
Although it knew that it would vanish soon.
How wonderful, I thought, at least to hear you
Abandoned, I have long longed to be near you
And find long lost refuge in a world.
I saw the truth of it within your eyes
And blessed the dream that ends but never dies.

Stewart Ashton (13)
Harris School, Rugby

My Poem

When you've got a family like mine
You surely would not mind
They would cheer you on at any game
All the way until you walk through the hall of fame.
They would teach you something new every day
And help you find success in every way.
They make sure you are comfortable were you are
Whether you are in a house or a car.
They teach you wrong from right
And persuade you to keep your dreams in sight.
They wipe your tears away when you are sad
And calm you down when you get mad.
Thank you family for all that you do,
I don't know where I would be if it weren't for you.
They make you feel better when you are blue
And whisper in your ear, 'I love you!'

Reiss Boon (14)
Harris School, Rugby

What Matters To You

What matters to me
Might not matter to you
A supportive family
And good friends
They do not judge whatever I've done
Wrong or right they won't give me a fright!
Whatever the weather rain or shine
A warm cosy home is mine
What matters to you
Might not matter to me.

Robert Scott (13)
Harris School, Rugby

What Matters To Me

The things I'm about to tell you
Are things quite important you see,
Things you may or may not agree with
But that doesn't matter to me.

My family is important
My friends are too,
The times we have, the love we share,
The things that feel brand new.

Other items that matter
Are silly things like my stuff,
My appearance, make-up and a lovely warm bed
And the incredible marshmallow fluff.

Things that aren't so personal
Not as personal as my name
But my home, my street, my town, my country
Their importance is the same.

I could go on forever
But forever is a very long time
Why don't you say what matters to you
As you've heard about mine.

Hannah Morgan (14)
Harris School, Rugby

Life

Fighting, killing, smoking, drugs and life.
Fighting doesn't make the world a better place.
Killing doesn't make you a better person.
Smoking doesn't make you happy.
Drugs don't make you healthy or fit.
But life is something special you only live once.

Bronte Wrist (12)
Harris School, Rugby

What Matters To Me . . . Is The Music I Like

You say Lady GaGa, I say Motley Crue
You say pop, I say rock
You say JLS, I say Nirvana
You say Madonna, I say Green Day.

Heavy metal rules, pop sucks
Punk rules, R 'n' B sucks
Grunge rules, rap sucks
Glam rules, indie . . . well, some of it's okay.

Awesome music vids, sick songs
Vocals and guitars
Drums and bass
Concerts and clothing styles.

You say Girls Aloud, I say Guns 'n' Roses
You say X Factor, I say Slipknot
You say American Idol, I say Bullet For My Valentine
You say Michael Jackson, I say Metallica.

I love music, music's my life,
I'd be nothing without music.

Shay McNair (14)
Harris School, Rugby

What Matters To Me

Family matters to me,
Brothers, sisters, mums and dads,
That's what matters to me,
Pets and grandparents,
That's definitely what matters to me.

Food matters to me,
Fruit, crisps, chocolate and veg,
That's what matters to me,
Lollies and biscuits,
Those especially matter to me.

Education matters to me,
Books English, maths and science,
That's what matters to me,
Art and drama,
They so matter to me.

Life matters to me,
Heartbeats, hair, eyes and mouth,
That's what matters to me,
Blood and hair,
They're all the things that matter to me,
Without life, the other things would not matter to me.

Dominique Beards (13)
Harris School, Rugby

Home Sweet Home!

Home sweet home,

My house is sweet
But can be sour
My house is quiet
But can be loud
From my sister's room, that is.

My house is light
But can be dark
My house is full of happy memories
But also bad ones.

My house is full of laughter
But also sometimes tears
My house smells delicious dinner cooking
But not always such a nice smell.

This is my house,
Home sweet home!

Joe Barnes (12)
Harris School, Rugby

My Family

My dad's not bad; he cheers me up when I'm sad.
My mum's not young but she puts food in my tum.
My grandad's not mad; with him I'm never sad.
My aunt's sometimes late, but she didn't miss her first date.
My uncle's bald, that makes him look old.
My cousin's hyper; I say he's like the Pied Piper.
My cousin's a teen, she's a bit in-between.

Dan Malin (13)
Harris School, Rugby

The World

The world is a magnificent place,
Full of lots of animals,
But we are the main race.
It has beautiful bright flowers,
One of every colour,
But then it has its rain showers.

This beautiful Earth has its downs,
Nothing is ever perfect
With pollution all around.
Still we can see the bright of day,
The sun shining like a light.
Yet we still pray,
When our world will be perfect and perfect forever.

Jessica Young (11)
Harris School, Rugby

Home

Home is a place where we let our hair fall.
Home is our place to be ourselves.
Home is a place to cry and shout
But home is our place to do our thing and nothing else.

Home is a place to feel free
To jump up and down with glee.
Where we can dream happy dreams
Or eat our favourite flavoured ice cream.

There will always be a place in my heart
Where my home will always be
Even when I move out
It will always be home to me.

Jade Smith (13)
Harris School, Rugby

Friends

They mean the world to me,
They help me through the day,
They're there for me when I need them,
And they mean so much to me,
We fall out over stupid things,
But we always make it anything,
I can tell them anything,
They're always by my side,
We fall out over things that are nothing,
Still we stick together always,
Some are not so close,
But still mean a lot,
Through tears and heartaches,
There is always a shoulder to cry on,
I would do anything for them,
They are like family to me.

Holly Burgess (14)
Harris School, Rugby

Rugby

Rugby is the thing I love
Even though some prefer the bath tub.
It makes me grin, it makes me smile,
I just want to play it all the while
Even though sometimes it hurts after.
I never want to stop because it fills me with laughter,
So this is why I love the game.

Mitchell Hughes (13)
Harris School, Rugby

My Home

Home is a place to rest,
I help and try to do my best.
Home is where I stay
When my cousin's come over to play.
Home is a roof over my head,
Where at night I go to bed.
Home is where you can have sleepovers
Then we go out and find a clover.
Home is where everything happens.

Alana John (13)
Harris School, Rugby

The Big Grey Fluffy Fat Cat

In the morning
He purrs tenderly
He stretches elegantly
He asks for food hungrily
That's the big, grey, fluffy, fat cat.

During the day
He waits and waits, tranquil and low
He pounces belligerent and war-like
He struts, meticulous and king
That's the big, grey, fluffy, fat cat.

The night draws in
He comes in peaceful.
He sits on the sofa all snug and warm
He asks for love secure and soft
That's the life of the big, grey, fluffy cat.

Connor Mellet (12)
Harris School, Rugby

Earth Is A Volatile Place

Earth is a volatile place
There's conflict and wars
There's terrorist attacks and nuclear weaponry
There's infectious diseases affecting us all
Epidemics which don't respect any borders
Environmental disasters affecting us all.

Earth is a volatile place
There's tornadoes and hurricanes which twirl and swirl
Causing destruction across the world
There's earthquakes and tsunamis that can sweep you off your feet
Fires and floods that cause devastation
Threats of meteor attacks and even alien invasion,
Earth is a volatile place.

Himesh Parmar (12)
Harris School, Rugby

Family And Friends

My family is mad,
But my mum makes sure no one is sad.
I have three sisters and one brother,
All from the same mother.
My friends mean the world to me,
Forever and ever we'll be.
Sleepovers and parties until the end,
Text messaging enter, click, send.
I'll never have to worry as someone will always be there,
Whether I'm happy, sad, excited or scared,
I don't know what I'd do without my family and friends.

Aimee Martin (13)
Harris School, Rugby

Winter

Every person is hiding,
In their warm, cosy houses,
While animals are cold and lonely,
Out in the snow.

Every creature is hiding,
In the cold depths of winter,
With mountains of food supplies,
Keeping them alive through the cold winter.

Every flower is hiding,
From the cold air that freezes them to death,
None come out whilst the icy weather is about,
As the weather warms the buds turn and sprout ready for the next spring.

Every living thing is hiding,
As the winter closes,
The buds appear,
Soon it will be spring when the fields will be filled with wild roses and beautiful daffodils.

Patrick Challen (11)
Harris School, Rugby

My Family

Fun to hang around with and always there for you
And in any time of aspiration, they can understand and fit in your shoe
Models and popstars can never replace the love they have for you
In any type of circumstances they can somehow help you through
Loving, protective, understanding and helpful – well what do you expect?
They want the best for you!
Young to old, they will always love you! You fall out, you get together again.
No one can take away the pure love they have for you.

Jamie James (10)
Harris School, Rugby

My Rabbits

My rabbits are Bertie and Bruce,
They drive me around like they're a mousse,
When I go and see them they always jump,
They are two very big lumps.

Bertie is mine, he will always be,
He loves everyone especially me,
He always washes Bruce,
He will never set loose.

Bruce is Alex's, he loves him lots,
He has got some very brown dots,
He is very playful,
Listening to the rain fall.

Ellie Langhorn (12)
Harris School, Rugby

What Matters To Me

What matters to me might not matter to you,
But I don't care about things that aren't true.

I care about football which matters to me.
Taekwondo matters to me because it's good,
It's a lot better than Christmas pud.

My family matters to me because they care
Although that's not rare.
My friends matter to me because they support,
They like to help and like to share.

Troy Loveridge (11)
Harris School, Rugby

Remember Those Soldiers

As we tend to those in pain,
We look upon those who died in vain.
Ever silent lay those reaped souls,
Where bullets have left subtle holes.
Weeping and sorrow in every direction,
On their faces a ghostly reflection.
All around lay the dead,
Their bodies painted with their own bloodshed.
My comrade's faces are a pale white,
But their haunting eyes as dark as the night.
Remember those soldiers that are no more,
You and me they fought and died for.

Jake Richardson (12)
Harris School, Rugby

My Bedroom

What would I do without it?
Nothing, I see it every day and every night.
Where I have dreams and nightmares,
Where I can hide away in the corner when I'm scared.

The door reads 'Keep Out!'
And that's what is meant.
It is there for a reason
So you better stick to it.

It's where I go to bed at night
And wake up in the morning.
What would I be without it?
Nothing.

Carolina Trincão (12)
Harris School, Rugby

What Matters To Me . . .

I make a difference
I speak kind words
I never lose patience
And I'm always heard.

I stand out from the rest
I do good things
I try my best
At whatever life brings.

I'm here to listen
Wherever you need
When your eyes start to glisten
I'll do the good deed.

I'm willing to give
To lend a helping hand
To change the way I live
And obey your every command.

I tend to smile
To have a happy face
To wait for a while
Then find a better place.

Until the end
I know what's right
I'll stay true to my friends
And hold on tight.

So this is the story
It's the only way
To have new found glory
And to make him stay.

Even if I fail
The people I defend
This one sad tale
Will come to an end.

I now can see
It's okay to cry
What matters to me
Is I kissed him goodbye.

Georgie Clark (14)
Harris School, Rugby

What Matters To Me

The world,
Being a better place,
No racism and hatred
It shouldn't matter about your race.

The future,
No one knows what it holds.
Ambitions and dreams,
They slowly start to unfold.

The people that matter to me,
What could I do without them?
Friends and family,
They always support you to the end.

Dancing is also everything to me,
The only thing I've stuck with.
A way to express myself,
Heart pounding on stage but still,
Enjoying every minute.

Nicky Tattal (13)
Harris School, Rugby

What Matters To Me

W onderful memories
H appy and sad
A re all
T hat matter to me

M y goal is to be in control of my life
A favourite colour of mine is green
T he other is purple
T he thrill for speed can sometimes scare me, but
E very time I see a sheep I smile
R oxy and Jade are my canine friends
S illy and fun, they keep me entertained

T he one thing most important to me is my sister
O ne of my favourite hobbies is building Lego models

M y last supper would be mussels, calamari and pizza
E very May I see the trees turn green and present wrapping all over the floor!

Ned Morley-Cottrell (11)
Harris School, Rugby

A Bit About Me

S o you want to know a bit about me
O n the Xbox I can't be beat
N othing much is what I do
N ot many songs I don't like
Y ou now know a little bit about me

H odder is my last name
O n my bike I normally am
D oing nothing but riding round
D on't Liverpool FC deserve a million pounds?
E verywhere I go I'm never normally alone because
R iding solo isn't my thing.

Sonny Hodder (11)
Harris School, Rugby

My Jeep

My jeep was built in 1944,
By the Americans to use in the war.
That means it's sixty-six years old,
I think it's time its story was told.

When it was bought by me and Dad,
It was looking very old and sad.
The paint was worn and there was rust,
Some of it crumbled and turned into dust.

We worked real hard and lots of hours,
We rubbed and sprayed and used our powers.
We had to take it all apart,
And from the beginning had to start.

Each piece was treated with loving care,
We worked in every hour spare.
Eventually she was back together,
But would it start in any weather?

Hooray! At last she's started,
And I know we will never be parted.
I hope she doesn't break down,
Or me and Dad will have a frown.

Tom Truslove (11)
Harris School, Rugby

What Matters About Me?

W hy it matters about me you may ask,
H opefully this poem will make you understand,
A bout me and,
T he things that matter.

M ates and their friendships,
A nd the good times we have,
T eamwork and leadership,
T alking and listening,
E veryone that has a positive impact on me and,
R ealising my goals in life,
S tretching my abilities to the limit.

A lso my loving family,
B rother love especially,
O ther people treating me as I treat them,
U nderstanding, feeling and seeing,
T he world that surrounds me.

M ost of all, the sports I play with,
E nthusiasm, energy and pleasure.

Daniel Hood (11)
Harris School, Rugby

Music

What matters to you?
Music is life
Breath and soul
A slicing knife
Or soothing warmth
Lyrics laced with fire
The melody burns
With heartfelt desire.
It is everlasting
Personal and secret
Clutching memories past.
With holding emotions
Unlocking iron chains
Like a melody potion.
It freeing the whole
Like a captive bird
Releasing a soul.

Beth Gillin (14)
Harris School, Rugby

Northampton Saints

The floodlights blaze,
The match kicks off.
The tackles go in,
The players go down.
Players run the ball up the pitch
And they're praying they don't get hit.
Tries awarded,
Conversions kicked.
Yellow cards given,
Players in the bin.
Whilst the crowd are cheering and singing,
A scrum takes place, the players are heaving.
After a while the match comes to an end.

Jack Wallace (11)
Harris School, Rugby

Narcissistic

Grin and bear it,
Sorry!
I cannot share it.
Spent hours with my reflection –
For I'm a slave. Perfection.

So I'll sit up all night and pray
So tomorrow
I'm ten times more beautiful
Than I am today.

Annah Butt (16)
Highams Park School, London

Definition Of Ride Or Die!

Though I stand before a mirror
I refuse to reflect on what has happened in the last couple of years
Because it has taken me the last couple of years to realise that I may have a phobia of myself
Which would explain why I muffle out the sound of my inner being crying out for help
She is so drunk with pain yet I front such a believable smile you would think she's sober

And as the process of human diffusion takes place
People come and go as they please
Taking from her life what they feel they need
Time takes its toll
I grow older, yet she does not progress.

She has been raped by the struggles of life and I am the bastardly production
The illegitimate child
My father's misfortune and my mother's lack of understanding
And the worse thing is, that those who claim to know me best know nothing.

I am the black and white photocopy of the prototype
She has been used to the point of exhaustion that she cannot be exposed to just anyone.

So when they drop the line
I want to get to know, I ask in which way
How can the handle the real me
When I know they would rather f*** the fake.

But over the years there have been few who have caught a glimpse of Jennifer.

So if I have constantly reminded you of how much you mean to me
Then be reassured that in years' time, I will still be standing by your side
Because your friendship is what I consider the real definition of ride or die.

Jennifer Pearl Johnson
Highams Park School, London

The Haunted House

I am frozen,
Completely terrified,
Listening intently,
I'm absolutely petrified!

I hear:
Nails scraping,
Feet shuffling,
Eerie groans,
Bizarre snuffling.

Knives rattling,
Floors creaking,
Quiet mumbling,
Doors squeaking.

I eventually muster the courage
Courage to venture around.
I grab a heavy cricket bat
Not making a single sound.

And do you know what?
All that scraping and squeaking
And all this noise on noise,
Can you guess what it was?
Little sister with her toys.

Kaitlyn Festa (11)
Highcrest Community School, High Wycombe

A Happy Birthday

I'm dreaming of a happy birthday
Presents swarming in.
Birthday cards and chocolate buttons
And a golden ring.
Yeah! I am a day older
But nothing has changed
Except the smile on my face.

Krislin Browne (12)
Highcrest Community School, High Wycombe

The Castle Of Ghosts and Ghouls

The big scary castle loomed ahead,
Oh how I wish I was still in bed!
It was a huge building taller than wide,
I just wanted to go home and quietly hide.

We went to sign our names in blood,
By trudging through the revolting mud.
We heard the screeching of bats,
And the scurrying sound of rats,
Outside the castle of ghosts and ghouls.

The inside of the castle was more shocking than out,
For it had disgusting dead bodies about.
There were spiders crawling left and right,
But the truly scary creatures come only at night.

Now I've told you about the castle of ghosts and ghouls,
Anybody who enters is an unbelievable fool!

Sania Tahir (11)
Highcrest Community School, High Wycombe

Seasons

S o many flowers bloom
P eople enjoy the wonderful weather
R elaxing on such hot days
I nteresting ideas which help us play
N ever shall we get bored
G reat games solve the problem!

S chool is finished and holidays begin
U sing all the time to laugh and play
M any magical mysteries happen
M ost go on holiday
E ven if you can't see your friend
R elaxing can never end.

A ll the leaves are on the floor
U pon the path where I can play
T ogether with my families and friends
U sing the leaves again and again
M any have lost their crisp and crunch
N ever have they lost their fun

W ith snow falling here and there
I ncluding on rooftops and on my hair
N ever ending fun and joy
T hen winter has come
E nding autumn for good
R elying on us to play until spring!

Saira Azhar (11)
Highcrest Community School, High Wycombe

Snow

See the shimmering snowflakes
Falling from the sky
On roofs and gardens
Smooth and glistening they lie.

I look in the garden
Where grass once was green
Layered by snowflakes
It can no longer be seen.

Katie Willoughby (11)
Highcrest Community School, High Wycombe

Brown Bear

B ig Barry brown bear
R eally fluffy
O ver the moon when he found McFlurry
W anting more all the time
N ever full when watching crime

B ellyache can occur when
E ating fur
A fter stomach pains he catches food with his
R ake like claws.

Adam O'Toole (11)
Highcrest Community School, High Wycombe

Halloween

The wind whistles through the trees.
Everyone screaming, shouting and playing,
All the children buzzing with laughter,
All the houses with lit pumpkins at their door
Shining brightly in the night.

Orange, red, black, colours all around,
Red blood dripping from people's mouths.
Children running, shouting, demanding sweets
Bags full of candy treats
That they all want to eat!

Everyone all dressed up,
Vampires, monsters, big furry things
All very scary.
For some too much
Little kids cry and scream,
And hide under their beds thinking
That the things outside might
Be the living dead!

Fireworks glisten in the night sky,
Colourful and loud, a great celebration.
It's always fun on Halloween!

Jacob Creswick (11)
Highcrest Community School, High Wycombe

Remember Me?

Remember me?
I was the girl who was your friend
Until the Devil changed you
Into a different person
Right at the end.

I feared you right at the start
Of each and every day,
Wondering with tears
With whom and what to play.

I was the one in the middle
When you kicked my feelings about,
The person who would always be
Hurt and left out.

But how different is the change
After years have passed by,
Like a vicious snake attacking
In order for it to survive.

I'm taller and stronger,
I'm two stones more in weight.
All of a sudden, I'm very well-liked
With no problems, with no pain.

But held in the back of my lovely brain
Is the memory of much pain.
Instead of revenge and justice
I'd rather be friends again,
Me and you.

Rahima Islam (11)
Highcrest Community School, High Wycombe

Life In School

Go in school, passing the old man Paul. Registration.
Then all starts to fall apart.
Tony twitches, Jordan's boredom, Stefan stares,
Chloe likes Tom (as if he cares).

Maths first lesson, sit next to my friend.
Not next to the bully, George, amen.
What is 5+5? I have no idea.
My best friend doesn't tell me, what a nice peer.

ICT next, the lesson of the best.
Turn computer on and logged in,
I start to begin worrying about my work,
I finished off and typed, 'He suddenly got stabbed by a dirk.'

Break! Thank God!
I shuffled over to Jake and gave him a shock.
I then ran away into the misty fade.

English now! The classwork I do is very foul.
Drawing scattered, writing splattered.
The book is extremely wet.
I should not have taken that life-risking bet.

Art introduced.
Work unreduced, detentions here, detentions there
Oh! The teachers just don't care.

Lunchtime is here! I hear everyone cheer!
I sit to eat my lunch; it is all in a bunch.
Bread on tomato on potato on lettuce on onion on bread. A mouthful.

Science, last lesson. We learn about bats, how they eat rats.
How they sleep upside down,
How some of them are extremely brown.

Registration again. Tony groans, Jordan sleeps, Stefan stares
Tom likes Chloe (as if she cares).

Time to go home,
I start to groan
This is a normal day at school,
It will never be cool.

Lamar Edwards (12)
Highcrest Community School, High Wycombe

Snow

Snow is falling from the sky
Piling up in enormous mounds.
School is closed for the day,
Everyone runs outside to play.

Snowmen are made so very, very high,
We put the eyes and mittens and scarves.
It's finished and done
And there it stands right in front.

Then we have a snowball fight
Which turns out really fine.
Everybody hides away
Except for me and Ray.

Almost over is the day
Everyone walks away
As the snow falls, so does the sun,
Time to go in, the day is done.

Husna Malik (11)
Highcrest Community School, High Wycombe

The Abandoned House

All I could hear was petrifying screams,
From the souls that were left behind.
The smell was unbearable,
Like decaying bodies with hint of blood.
As I walked in, cobwebs brushed against my hair.
I was so frightened!
Anything could be inside!

Aleisha Starkey (11)
Highcrest Community School, High Wycombe

War

My friends and allies fell about me
For a pointless cause,
The moans of pain echoing in my head,
Soon ceased and restored to the silence of the dead,
The bullets from machine guns ending people's lives,
The explosions from bombs catapulting friends and men I never knew,
The wet mud clinging to me and never letting go,
Slowing me down, draining my strength,
Bodies of boys younger than seventeen,
Decaying and rotting, never to go places they'd never been.

Matthew Snudden (12)
Highcrest Community School, High Wycombe

Walking

As the winter winds dance with the trees,
He carries on walking.

As springtime blossoms,
He carries on walking.

As the scorching summer sun rises in the sky,
He carries on walking.

As the autumn leaves blow,
He carries on walking.

As he faces the ever changing elements,
He carries on walking.

Carries on walking
To find his home.

Adam Lipinski (11)
Highcrest Community School, High Wycombe

The Blissful Beach

Sand
Sand which runs blissfully through your fingers like stroking wool.

Sea
The sea tediously drifting back and forth along the shore,
The waves
Lashing at the water beneath.

Laughter
Laughter which runs through your body and tingles you with happiness.

Freshness
Smelling the freshness from the sea which makes your soul feel at ease.

Shells
Shells washed up on the shore
Like broken bits of rainbow.

Sun
The sun glinting on the sea as if there were diamonds shining from the depths.

Toni Haywood (12)
Highcrest Community School, High Wycombe

A Summer's Night

I walked down the gleaming path
Waiting, just waiting, for a summer's night.

As the gracious moon rises from its prison
I gleam upon its mysterious beauty as if it was staring right at me.

As the gliding glory gleams right at me
Its only heart's desire is to escape its eternal prison.

Bienhaneen Hussain (11)
Highcrest Community School, High Wycombe

Primal Fear

Hurry, hurry, keep running, don't stop
You might feel tired but don't let yourself drop.
I run round the corner in the dead of night
Remembering to keep all of me out of sight.

The footsteps of my pursuer are all I can hear
I think, hurry up they're getting so near.
Suddenly I stop and my heart starts to pound
With the fear rising in me I slowly look round.

I peer through the gloom
With a strong sense of doom.
That's the moment I wake up in bed
I realise it was all in my head.

Charlotte Rumsey (11)
Highcrest Community School, High Wycombe

Tarmac Is Black

Tarmac is black, it is very sticky
It sticks to my back because it is icky
We can run on it, walk on it, dive on it, fall on it
Kick on it, throw on it, lick on it, sew on it
Sit on it, climb on it, hit on it, mime on it
I tried to swim in it; I can't get out of it
So I'm stuck in some muck!

Joe Andrews (11)
Liskeard School & Community College, Liskeard

My Family

Like people say, you can choose your friends but not your family
I found myself to be in the best family ever.

My mum brought me up to this world
By carrying me in her belly
But her carrying didn't stop there
She also had to take care of me
'You were hard to control,' she told me
But she never regretted having me
And told me I was the apple of her eye.

I also have a dad
Who makes me happy when I am sad
And treats me just like a princess
My dad is my saviour
He is my hero
Who makes me feel happy
When I am next to zero.

I have two tiny siblings, a brother and a sister
Who I love most dearly
Through every scratch and every blister.

I have a family
Who loves me
That's why I love them
Because they are always there for me!

Samrawit Russom (12)
Mount Carmel RC Girls' School, London

That Doesn't Matter To Me

All those girls want to be first
To buy that brand new Prada purse
Everyone at school calls me a freak
If I don't have a bit of Paul's Boutique
But that doesn't matter to me

When they come to school, they think they're foreign
Because they're wearing a shirt by Ralph Lauren
They would go up to their parents and nag and nag
If they don't get a bright pink Gucci bag
But that doesn't matter to me

I wouldn't be included in a game of hopscotch
If I'm not wearing a shiny blue Chanel watch
Everyone would leave the room
If they can't smell Dolce & Gabana perfume
But that doesn't matter to me

I'm not worried about the stuff they wear
The jewellery, the shoes or the style of their hair
I come to school to learn, have a chat
Which is why I don't come looking like that

What matters to me is the way I'm dressed
It's only school, it's not a test
All those girls should just give it a rest
Because I know that I look the best.

Olivia Smith (12)
Mount Carmel RC Girls' School, London

Puberty

The day my body changed was a brand new start for me
My hormones were like fire burning into me,
I had to stop this now,
Spots appeared out of nowhere and gradually got bigger,
Suddenly I had an attraction for the opposite sex.

The day my body changed was a brand new start for me
My twenty-eight day cycle called period started quickly,
The pain in my tummy grew immensely,
All of a sudden I became hairy,
My hormones started acting crazy,
But it was too late to change me.

The day my body changed was a brand new start for me
My hips widened,
I was changed completely
I was a new woman, all because of puberty.

Toyin Olukosi (13)
Mount Carmel RC Girls' School, London

I Love Make-Up

I love make-up because it makes me look nice just like you.
I love make-up; yes I do - put it on just like you.
It's not nice when you look like a clown to me.
I love make-up; yes I do - put it on just like you.
I am beautiful not like you, ha, ha, ha, you're a clown.
I love make-up; yes I do - put it on just like you.
Oh no, I look like a clown - not like you, you are beautiful
I love make-up; yes I do - put it on just like you.

Jade Mohamed (12)
Mount Carmel RC Girls' School, London

What The Yellow Star Means To Me

Pride goes before a fall,
Shamefully I realised the shame of my religion,
The only thing of my pride
Was taken away
To be humiliated, I hear my mournful heart
Mourn in despair.
I feel isolated, discriminated.
Heartbroken, stabbed at the heart.
I am innocent, a girl of ten years knowing nothing.

I stare, scared at the eyes that compassed me
And against me.
I see, I feel the highness of their hatred at one stare.
What did I do? Why am I rejected?
Am I the world's most hated girl?
Glaring at my dirty, torn, yellow star
That contrasted with my worn brown shirt,
Not able to speak
For it spoke for itself, for I am only a girl of ten.

Children and adults stare at me in disgust
Like a rat, a rotten rat.
My faith has brought me to a fall,
My dignity still stands firm
For it is who I am.
They can't take my humble soul.
I am different; they can steal my pride,
For inside I am like a roaring lion, undefeated
They glare at me under the rising sun as a slave
To be mocked and cast on the outside
But inside my heart rejoices.
I am a girl of only ten,
My pride was taken from me.

Nkemjika Peace-be Ben-Nwankwo (11)
Mount Carmel RC Girls' School, London

Try To Live Life Like I Do

Another day at school,
Another day full of misery and sadness,
Hours feel like weeks,
And the days feel like years,
I wear my dull grey uniform,
Unsure if I was ready for another dull day at school,
I walk to the class in the dull grey morning, lonely and afraid,
As they stare straight at me with smirks on their faces,
Please God not again,
Bam!
I look at my blood in their hands,
And the pain that I feel,
But wait,
What did I do wrong?
They think it's cool to be cruel,
But they don't know how it feels to be me,
I wish I could become a baby again,
With no worries, no fears, no stress and no bullies,
I wish I could just go to sleep and never wake up again,
That's how it feels to be me.

Khadija Khan (12)
Mount Carmel RC Girls' School, London

Me, Myself And My Baby

Little girl, little girl,
You naughty little girl
You did it once, you did it twice
Now you have to pay the price.
Why oh why oh why didn't you use a condom?

Seventy-two hours of labour not a sound not a whisper
Her boyfriend was not there
She hates him, she hates him, she hates her life
Why oh why oh why didn't you use a condom?

Now she can't be who she used to be,
She can't go to school without someone looking at her
It's hard for her to look for clothes she was size 10 now she is size 16
Why oh why oh why didn't you use a condom?

Now the baby has arrived
Should she keep it or should she leave it?
Should she love it or should she hate it?
She's just so confused, she has a new life
She is a mother but is still just a little girl.

Alezandra Stevens-Dyal (11)
Mount Carmel RC Girls' School, London

They Roam The Streets Like Bad Boys

Pam-pom, pam-pom, a familiar sound
A police car speeding past.
But no one takes any notice.
Where's it going? What is wrong?
No one really cares,
They roam the streets like bad boys.

Walking the dog at night, take care
A lady says, 'Don't go down there!
A gang is out with a nasty dog.
It looks vicious,' she says.
'Don't go down there.'
They roam the streets like bad boys.

A boy is running through the estate.
'Help! Help!' he cries.
He can hardly breathe.
'They're going to get me, they've got a knife.'
They roam the streets like bad boys.

A car is missing,
The police are called.
They patrol the streets
Suddenly they see a fire.
'What's that?'
'It's the stolen car.'
It's burnt out and the air is full of smoke.
They roam the streets like bad boys.

A car goes past
It's really fast
But it's not going anywhere
Round the block and back again
They roam the streets like bad boys.

Gemma Cooper (12)
Mount Carmel RC Girls' School, London

Angels' Wings

Angels' wings are beautiful things,
Like so many butterflies,
I want to fly free.

Angel dust,
Glittering, sparkling,
Oh how I must try and gather.

Angels' feet so soft and sweet,
Like the clouds they walk on.
I want to walk free.

Angels full of comforting love
And bright celestial light,
Entering our world from above
Helping to put it right.

Angels' hands are the golden bands,
Which keep the loved ones united.
I want to be free.

Fluttering, sparkling,
Twinkling, shimmering,
Flying angels.
Glittering, glimmering.

Take me to where I belong
Take me to happiness
I want to be free.

Faster than light
Through the cosmos so high
Fulfilling their mission
To be by your side.

Take my hand
And walk with me
Please help me
I want to be free
I want to go to Heaven.

Cansel Gok (12)
Mount Carmel RC Girls' School, London

Family

My mum cares for me
My brother takes the key
He drinks all my drinks
And takes all my things
But I love my brother
My mum and me
As we are one happy family.

My mum is the cream to my hair
My brother's the boy who's always downstairs
We fight all the time
Although that's no crime
But I love my brother
My mum and me
As we are one happy family.

Milen Rosum (12)
Mount Carmel RC Girls' School, London

That's What Friends Are For

Friends are nice
Friends are cool
That's what friends are for.

Someone to talk to
Someone to play with
Someone to tell your problems to
That's what friends are for.

We would have arguments
And have our ups and downs
We will still be friends
That's what friends are for

We would get hurt
But chin up
That's what friends are for.

Paige Cassidy (11)
Mount Carmel RC Girls' School, London

Why Me? Why Now?

We meet on a cold Monday morning
Also the bus was cold and boring
You said hello then went away
When I looked round you had nothing to say.
Why me? Why now?

I see you every day,
You're with your friends who are funny and nice,
Also stubborn and annoying.
Why me? Why now?

Your friend, who is a girl, she tells me to go away
So I think she wants us to be apart.
But I don't want this,
Why me? Why now?

You say hello on Facebook
But you never say hello face to face.
I feel like she's keeping us apart.
She's always all over you but you push her away
So I guess that says you don't want her you want me.
Why me? Why now?

Georgia Wallace (13)
Mount Carmel RC Girls' School, London

Love

Love is like a diamond it can be broken in seconds.
Love is like a heart that never stops beating.
When love is in you it can never come out
Only when your relationship dies it is free again.

You can give love to everyone around you
But the only person you want is who's beside you.
Beside you when you cry, beside you when you need them,
Beside you when you love them.
People say that love is simple but love is like a dream that never stops,
That's how you know you love them,
Don't let your relationship die.

Love is like a diamond that can be broken in seconds
Once it's broken you can never bring it back
Only true love does that.
The person will love you, care for you,
But the only words you can say are I love you.

Lara Gomes (13)
Mount Carmel RC Girls' School, London

True Friendship Never Dies

I have a true friend
Who can understand you,
Know that they'll never judge you,
Can help you in situations when life gets tough.
That's true friendship that will never die.

A true friend that can make you laugh even when you're down,
Make you smile all the time,
Feeling happy because you know you've got a true friend on your side.
That's true friendship that will never die.

When you have your ups and downs with them
But you both find a way to forgive and forget.
A true friend who will never let anything
Come between the two of you,
Who will ignore the rumours and stick by you no matter what.
That's a true friendship that will never die.

A true friendship is supposed to be rock solid
Knowing completely everything about each other
Treating each other like sisters,
That's a true friendship that will never die.

Chanté Sylvester (13)
Mount Carmel RC Girls' School, London

Living Or Dying?

Every day is a fight to stay alive
When a new one comes
It's always you with the knife,
'Please stop, stop crime,' I want to cry.

When I live
I want to die
Because I know it's coming . . .
But why?
'Please stop, stop crime,' I want to cry.

It's a new day
But I'm scared
I don't know what's coming my way
'Please stop, stop crime,' I want to cry.

My day is coming,
Please let it pass.
I want to know my future
Please let me last.
'Please stop, stop crime.' I want to cry.

Christiana Wynter (11)
Mount Carmel RC Girls' School, London

Grow Up

When I was born
Mum delivered good news
She has a baby girl
What will happen when I grow up?

When I was three
Dad bought me a doll
A Barbie head doll
What will happen when I grow up?

When I was five
My brother took me for the first day
As the door opens to my new school
What will happen when I grow up?

When I was eight
My family took me to Ghana
What will I see in Ghana?
Life in Ghana is so exotic
What will happen when I grow up?

When I was eleven
My sister took me to the open gates of
Mount Carmel RC Technology College
What will happen when I grow up?
You will have to wait and see.

Emma Winful (11)
Mount Carmel RC Girls' School, London

The Right To Be Safe

I walked down the street
Night has fallen
I'm shaking more than the trees are being blown
I wonder if I'm safe
Or I will get attacked
God protect us, we need to be safe!

Even walking through the day
The trees are spies,
They see and hear about what goes on
Families waiting patiently for their child to arrive home
God protect us, we need to be safe!

Hearing cries in the wood, cries of pain
The wood never hear cries of joy
The leaves worried of guiltiness
They choose to give their victims a blind eye
God protect us, we need to be safe!

Family grieving from horrid news
Some drink booze
To get rid of nasty memories
Others lock themselves up
Some go extremely to the top
God protect us, we need to be safe!

Stephanie Odidika (12)
Mount Carmel RC Girls' School, London

Love Hurts

I think I'm falling in love,
As we hold each other's hands,
My lips start to smile,
My head is in dreamland.
I think I'm falling in love,
As I hug him for so long,
My belly has butterflies,
Our love is just so strong.
I think I'm falling in love,
As he kisses me on the cheek,
My hands start to sweat,
My body feels all weak.
I think I'm falling in love,
When we kiss on lips,
My legs start to tremble,
As his hands fall to my hips.
I think I'm falling in love,
As he tells me I'm the one,
My heart thumps with excitement,
As we both look into the sun.
I think I'm falling in love,
But then I saw him with that girl,
My eyes start to water,
He told me I was his world.
I thought I was in love,
When I looked into his eyes,
But then my heart was broken,
Because of all his awful lies.

Agatha Xavier (12)
Mount Carmel RC Girls' School, London

It Must Be Right

They chat and chat
From day to night
Deciding on what to wear.
It *must* be right.

It gets quite annoying
For those who are unfortunate
To have an older sister
Who is forever stuck in her own world
Chatting to her friends.

Every week they go out shopping
And come back
With a whole load of worries.
It *must* be the age
My mum would say.

What should I wear?
What should I wear?
She would parrot to herself
As if it was a national crisis.

She would turn to me
Only for an opinion
But she would only go with her own decision.
It *must* be right.

I wonder a lot
Why she asks for my opinion
When she always ends up going with her own decision.

It *must* be right.

Shabnoor Ali (12)
Mount Carmel RC Girls' School, London

Appearance, What Does It Matter To You?

She sees herself in the mirror,
A beauty queen,
On the front cover of every magazine,
Appearance, what does it matter to you?
Style icon, flashing lights,
Movie star, front headlines.

Make-up, made up.
With Maybelline,
Took two hours to create this scene,
Pouting her lips, moving her hips,
Flittering false lashes, is she happy with this?
Appearance, what does it matter to you?

Behind her lies,
Stuck to a wall,
A camouflage of posters of who she adores,
Beckham, Aniston, Jolie and Berry,
Wishing to be as famous as these.
Appearance, what does it matter to you?

Feeling neglected, she chooses to be alone,
Her family worry about her,
To them it is nonsense,
Dressed in gold jeggings and a slinky tight top,
Three inch heels she can hardly walk in.
Appearance, what does it matter to you?

Zephania Osei-Bonsu (11)
Mount Carmel RC Girls' School, London

Lucky I Have A Family!

The golden sun shines,
Birds twitter, feeding their babies hearing their whines.
As you can see these are all love signs!

Lucky I have a family as protective as a shield,
Lucky I have a family who will protect me through thick and thin.

I shall never take my family for granted;
I have parents who will risk thier lives for me.
So listen to the touching things I have chanted!

Lucky I have a family as protective as a shield,
Lucky I have a family who will protect me through thick and thin.

This is why God put parents on the planet!
Mother's hugs are warm and caring
They are as graceful as doves, and bring our lives to a happier level.

Mothers are a part of us,
Father's mind full of frustration earning money for our education from when we are just eleven.
So stop being rude and start feeling like you're in Heaven.

Lucky I have a family as protective as a shield,
Lucky I have a family who will protect me through thick and thin.

Listen all teenagers, be respectful towards your parents!
Sweat trickled down my head as I hugged my mother - proctected from all evil.

Adwaa Choudhury (11)
Mount Carmel RC Girls' School, London

Please Someone Help Me!

The door is locked, I cannot breathe,
Please someone help me
There is no air in this sheltered life,
Please someone help me.
Release, relief is all I need,
Please someone help me.
Oh Lord, oh Lord, deliver me please,
Please someone help me.
If only I can smell the beautiful fresh air,
Please someone help me.
If only I can get proper education,
Please someone help me.
If only I can get out of this unhygienic factory,
Please someone help me.
I wonder, I wonder if I am the only young teenager without freedom,
Please someone help me.
The dim lights are shadowy and it is a blurred sight.
They are damaging my sight, I can't really see,
Please someone help me.
Whatever did I do to get into this dump?
Please someone help me.

Danielle Famiyesin (11)
Mount Carmel RC Girls' School, London

Billy Will . . .

Going to a trip with my school.
Don't want to.
Billy's coming.

Good day for some.
Not for all.

Going swimming today.
Don't want to.
Billy's coming.

Good day for some.
Not for all.

Getting a new phone today.
Don't want to.
Billy will get it.

Good day for some.
Not for all.

Walking home by myself today.
Don't want to.
Billy will rush me.

Good day for some.
Not for all.

Telling the teacher today.
I want to.
Billy will stop.

Lorissa Kaja (11)
Mount Carmel RC Girls' School, London

Dangerous Fun

We were bored, we were stupid
We thought it was fun
We thought it was funny
We were bored, we were stupid
We thought we were cool
We thought we were brave
We were bored, we were stupid.

A bridge so high
A bridge so tall
We were bored, we were stupid
A bridge too far from water
A bridge too far from safety
We were bored, we were stupid.

It was a rush
It was a risk
We were bored, we were stupid
It was something daring
It was something dumb
We were bored, we were stupid.

When it happened, it was a scream
When it happened, it was a nightmare
We were bored, we were stupid.
When she fell, we couldn't help
When she fell, she died
We were bored, we were stupid.

The water and the night are murderous
The water and the night are death-ridden
We were bored, we were stupid!

Megan-Alicia Jones (12)
Mount Carmel RC Girls' School, London

Featured Poets:
DEAD POETS
AKA Mark Grist & MC Mixy

Mark Grist and MC Mixy joined forces to become the 'Dead Poets' in 2008.

Since then Mark and Mixy have been challenging the preconceptions of poetry and hip hop across the country. As 'Dead Poets', they have performed in venues ranging from nightclubs to secondary schools; from festivals to formal dinners. They've appeared on Radio 6 Live with Steve Merchant, they've been on a national tour with Phrased and Confused and debuted their show at the 2010 Edinburgh Fringe, which was a huge success.

Both Mark and Mixy work on solo projects as well as working together as the 'Dead Poets'. Both have been Peterborough's Poet Laureate, with Mixy holding the title for 2010.

The 'Dead Poets' are available for workshops in your school as well as other events. Visit www.deadpoetry.co.uk for further information and to contact the guys!

Read on to pick up some fab writing tips!

Your WORKSHOPS

In these workshops we are going to look at writing styles and examine some literary techniques that the 'dead poets' use. Grab a pen, and let's go!

Rhythm Workshop

Rhythm in writing is like the beat in music. Rhythm is when certain words are produced more forcefully than others, and may be held for longer duration. The repetition of a pattern is what produces a 'rhythmic effect'. The word rhythm comes from the Greek meaning of 'measured motion'.

Count the number of syllables in your name. Then count the number of syllables in the following line, which you write in your notepad: 'My horse, my horse, will not eat grass'.

Now, highlight the longer sounding syllables and then the shorter sounding syllables in a different colour.

Di dum, di dum, di dum, di dum is a good way of summing this up.

You should then try to write your own lines that match this rhythm. You have one minute to see how many you can write!

Examples include:
'My cheese smells bad because it's hot'
and
'I do not like to write in rhyme'.

For your poem, why don't you try to play with the rhythm? Use only longer beats or shorter beats? Create your own beat and write your lines to this?

Did you know ... ?

Did you know that paper was invented in China around 105AD by Ts'ai Lun. The first English paper mill didn't open until 1590 and was in Dartford.

Rhyme Workshop

Start off with the phrase 'I'd rather be silver than gold' in your notepad. and see if you can come up with lines that rhyme with it -
'I'd rather have hair than be bald'
'I'd rather be young than be old'
'I'd rather be hot than cold'
'I'd rather be bought than sold'

Also, pick one of these words and see how many rhymes you can find:

Rose

Wall

Warm

Danger

What kinds of rhymes did you come up with? Are there differences in rhymes? Do some words rhyme more cleanly than others? Which do you prefer and why?

Onomatopoeia Workshop

Divide a sheet of A4 paper into 8 squares.

You then have thirty seconds to draw/write what could make the following sounds:

Splash	Ping
Drip	Bang
Rip	Croak
Crack	Splash

Now try writing your own ideas of onomatopoeia. Why might a writer include onomatopoeia in their writing?

Lists Workshop

Game - you (and you can ask your friends or family too) to write as many reasons as possible for the following topics:

Annoying things about siblings

The worst pets ever

The most disgusting ingredients for a soup you can think of

Why not try writing a poem with the same first 2, 3 or 4 words?

I am ...

Or

I love it when ...

Eg:

I am a brother

I am a listener

I am a collector of secrets

I am a messer of bedrooms.

Repetition Workshop

Come up with a list of words/ phrases, aim for at least 5. You now must include one of these words in your piece at least 6 times. You aren't allowed to place these words/ phrases at the beginning of any of the lines.

Suggested words/phrases:

Why

Freedom

Laughing

That was the best day ever

I can't find the door

I'm in trouble again

The best

Workshop POETRY 101

Below is a poem written especially for Poetry Matters, by MC Mixy.
Why not try and write some more poems of your own?

What is Matter?

© MC Mixy

What matters to me may not be the same things that matter to you
You may not agree with my opinion mentality or attitude
The order in which I line up my priorities to move
Choose to include my view and do what I do due to my mood
And state of mind
I make the time to place the lines on stacks of paper and binds
Concentrate on my artwork hard I can't just pass and scrape behind
Always keep close mates of mine that make things right
And even those who can't … just cos I love the way they can try
What matters to me is doing things the right way
It's tough this game of life we play what we think might stray from what others might say
In this world of individuality we all wanna bring originality
Live life and drift through casually but the vicious reality is
Creativity is unique
Opinions will always differ but if you figure you know the truth, speak
So many things matter to me depending on how tragically deep you wanna go
I know I need to defy gravity on this balance beam
As I laugh and breathe draft and read map the scene practise piece smash the beat and graphic release
Visual and vocal it's a standard procedure
Have to believe and don't bite the hand when it feeds ya

If you wanna be a leader you need to stay out of the pen where the sheep are
The things that matter to me are
My art and my friends
That will stay from the start to the end
People will do things you find hard to amend
Expect the attacks and prepare you gotta be smart to defend
I put my whole heart in the blend the mass is halved yet again
I'm marked by my pen a big fish fighting sharks of men
In a small pond
Dodging harpoons and nets hooks and predators tryna dismember ya
I won't let them I won't get disheartened I can fend for myself
As long as I'm doing what's important
I'm my mind where I'm supported is a just cause to be supporting
In these appalling hard times I often find myself falling when
Only two aspects of my life keep me sane and allow me to stand tall again
Out of all of them two is a small number
It's a reminder I remind ya to hold necessity and let luxury fall under
Try to avoid letting depression seep through
Take the lesson we actually need a lot less than we think we do
So what matters to you?
They may be similar to things that matter to me
I'm actually lacking the need of things I feel would help me to succeed
Though I like to keep it simple, I wanna love, I wanna breed
I'm one of many individuals in this world where importance fluctuates and varies
Things that matter will come and go
But the ones that stay for long enough must be worth keeping close
If you're not sure now don't watch it you'll know when you need to know
Me, I think I know now … yet I feel and fear I don't.

Turn overleaf for a poem by Mark Grist and some fantastic hints and tips!

Workshop POETRY 101

What Tie Should I Wear Today?

© Mark Grist

I wish I had a tie that was suave and silk and slick,
One with flair, that's debonair and would enchant with just one flick,
Yeah, I'd like that … a tie that's hypnotizing,
I'd be very restrained and avoid womanising,
But all the lady teachers would still say 'Mr Grist your tie's so charming!'
As I cruise into their classrooms with it striking and disarming.
At parents' evenings my tie's charm would suffice,
In getting mums to whisper as they leave 'Your English teacher seems nice!'

Or maybe an evil-looking tie - one that's the business,
Where students will go 'Watch out! Mr Grist is
on the prowl with that evil tie.'
The one that cornered Josh and then ripped out his eye.
Yeah no one ever whispers, no one ever sniggers,
Or my tie would rear up and you'd wet your knickers.
Maybe one girl just hasn't heard the warning,
Cos she overslept and turned up late to school that morning,
And so I'd catch her in my lesson yawning … oh dear.
I'd try to calm it down, but this tie's got bad ideas.
It'd size the girl up and then just as she fears,
Dive in like a serpent snapping at her ears.
There'd be a scream, some blood and lots and lots of tears,
And she wouldn't be able to yawn again for years.

Or maybe … a tie that everyone agrees is mighty fine
And people travel from miles around to gawp at the design
I'd like that … a tie that pushes the boundaries of tieware right up to the limit
It'd make emos wipe their tears away while chavs say 'It's wicked innit?'
and footy lads would stop me with 'I'd wear that if I ever won the cup.'
And I'd walk through Peterborough to slapped backs, high fives, thumbs up
While monosyllabic teenagers would just stand there going 'Yup.'

I don't know. I'd never be sure which of the three to try
As any decision between them would always end a tie.

Tips and Advice for PERFORMING Your Poem

So you've written your poem, now how about performing it. Whether you read your poem for the first time in front of your class, school or strangers at an open mic event or poetry slam, these tips will help you make the best of your performance.

Breathe and try to relax.

Every poet that reads in front of people for the first time feels a bit nervous, when you're there you are in charge and nothing serious can go wrong.

People at poetry slams or readings are there to support the poets. They really are!

If you can learn your poem off by heart that is brilliant, however having a piece of paper or notebook with your work in is fine, though try not to hide behind these.

It's better to get some eye contact with the audience. If you're nervous find a friendly face to focus on.

Try to read slowly and clearly and enjoy your time in the spotlight.

Don't rush up to the microphone, make sure it's at the right height for you and if you need it adjusted ask one of the team around you.

Before you start, stand up as straight as you can and get your body as comfortable as you can and remember to hold your head up.

The microphone can only amplify what what's spoken into it; if you're very loud you might end up deafening people and if you only whisper or stand too far away you won't be heard.

When you say something before your poem, whether that's hello or just the title of your poem, try and have a listen to how loud you sound. If you're too quiet move closer to the microphone, if you're too loud move back a bit.

Remember to breathe! Don't try to say your poem so quickly you can't find time to catch your breath.

And finally, **enjoy!**

Poetry FACTS

Here are a selection of fascinating poetry facts!

No word in the English language rhymes with 'MONTH'.

William Shakespeare was born on 23rd April 1564 and died on 23rd April 1616.

The haiku is one of the shortest forms of poetic writing.
Originating in Japan, a haiku poem is only seventeen syllables, typically broken down into three lines of five, seven and five syllables respectively.

The motto of the Globe Theatre was 'totus mundus agit histrionem' (the whole world is a playhouse).

The Children's Laureate award was an idea by Ted Hughes and Michael Morpurgo.

The 25th January each year is Burns' Night, an occasion in honour of Scotland's national poet Robert Burns.

Spike Milligan's 'On the Ning Nang Nong' was voted the UK's favourite comic poem in 1998.

Did you know *onomatopoeia* means the word you use sounds like the word you are describing – like the rain *pitter-patters* or the snow *crunches* under my foot.

'Go' is the shortest complete sentence in the English language.

Did you know rhymes were used in olden days to help people remember the news? Ring-o'-roses is about the Plague!

The Nursery Rhyme 'Old King Cole' is based on a real king and a real historical event. King Cole is supposed to have been an actual monarch of Britain who ruled around 200 A.D.

Edward Lear popularised the limerick with his poem 'The Owl and the Pussy-Cat'.

Lewis Carroll's poem 'The Jabberwocky' is written in nonsense style.

POEM – noun

1. a composition in verse, esp. one that is characterized by a highly developed artistic form and by the use of heightened language and rhythm to express an intensely imaginative interpretation of the subject.

Poetry TIPS

We have compiled some helpful tips for you budding poets...

In order to write poetry, read lots of poetry!

Keep a notebook with you at all times so you can write whenever (and wherever) inspiration strikes.

Every line of a poem should be important to the poem and interesting to read. A poem with only 3 great lines should be 3 lines long.

Use an online rhyming dictionary to improve your vocabulary.

Use free workshops and help sheets to learn new poetry styles.

Experiment with visual patterns - does your written poetry create a good pattern on the page?

Try to create pictures in the reader's mind - aim to fire the imagination.

Develop your voice. Become comfortable with how you write.

Listen to criticism, and try to learn from it, but don't live or die by it.

Say what you want to say, let the reader decide what it means.

Notice what makes other's poetry memorable. Capture it, mix it up and make it your own. (Don't copy other's work word for word!)

Go wild. Be funny. Be serious. Be whatever you want!

Grab hold of something you feel - anything you feel - and write it.

The more you write, the more you develop. Write poetry often.

Use your imagination, your own way of seeing.

Feel free to write a bad poem, it will develop your 'voice'.

Did you know ...?

'The Epic of Gilgamesh' was written thousands of years ago in Mesopotamia and is the oldest poem on record.

Alone

I lie alone
This very night
No friend
No family
No one in sight
Darkness surrounding me again tonight
What matters to me is being alone.

I cannot see my most hurtful fright
The rain
The cracks
The unmeaningful flash
What great relief I'm still alive
What matters to me is being alone.

My mask is off
My fears are here
The darkness there
Just can't see

I cannot claim what I fear the most
I cannot stop the unholy ghost
My fears are held so very close
What matters to me is being alone.

I scream, I yell
So very loud
Yet my voice isn't heard out loud
What matters to me is being alone
So help, I am alone.

Maria Babalola (11)
Mount Carmel RC Girls' School, London

Don't Take My Family Away From Me

The love and care for my family is like no other . . .

Don't take my family away from me.

The rice and chicken that my mum makes is like a restaurant meal made for one . . .

Don't take my family away from me.

The grand smile on my dad's face as he walks through the colossal door towards me and as he does this he calls me his little pumpkin . . .

Don't take my family away from me.

When I get home I see my bigger sisters working on their homework.
They work so hard and that is what I like about them.

Don't take my family away from me.

Finally I come to my annoying brothers,
They try so hard to annoy me especially when I am doing important homework. But that is what I love about them as they always make me laugh . . .

Don't take my family away from me and don't take them for granted.

Ore Olukoga (12)
Mount Carmel RC Girls' School, London

Underage

Why did she do it, was it pressure or was it true love?
Why did he do it, was it a laugh or was it true love?
She is only 16.

Now at the hospital she is in pain.
He has gone for a fag; will she ever see him again?
She is only 16.

Pushing and pushing, harder and harder, she is nearly in tears but where is the father?
He is outside getting some air wondering, do I really care?
She is only 16.

Now Mum is here fussing over the baby
While my dad is watching with a smile and I'm glad.
She is only 16.

The dad buggered off but I don't care,
I'll be fine with this cheeky mare.
She is only 16.

Even without the dad we will be fine,
The baby will always be mine.
She is only 16.

Colette McNamara (11)
Mount Carmel RC Girls' School, London

Exams

My mind is racing,
I've been revising,
All night long.

I'm up so early,
Relaxing in the bath,
Hoping my brain can remember this stuff.

Can I remember the maths I've been taught?
Tables, angles, multiples and more,
Can I remember to count to four?

My head is banging,
It's time to start,
Take a deep breath,
And count to four.

Lauren Hopson (11)
Mount Carmel RC Girls' School, London

My Family

The love, the happiness,
The family I will always love
Is right here in this room
Giving me love all the time.

They're pains but I love them.
They are always willing to help
Even if they're busy.
Giving me love all the time.

The smiling, the laughing,,
The happy vibe always in the room
Giving me love all the time.

They are all my family,
Always loving,
Always caring
Giving everyone love all the time.

Mali Swift-Wilson (11)
Mount Carmel RC Girls' School, London

It's Not My Phone!

She's playing with her phone while shopping.
He comes, grabs and runs!
I don't care as long as he don't take my phone.

She walks along the street, posing by each window,
Takes a photo of only her then he grabs and runs,
A sad face left on the street.
I don't care as long as he don't take my phone.

She's dancing along the street, not looking ahead then he grabs, runs.
I don't care as long as he don't take my phone.

I'm walking across the street with my new phone, texting and calling
Then he grabs, runs, I cry, I die.
Now I do care.

Tasnim Akter (12)
Mount Carmel RC Girls' School, London

I'm Only Myself

You want to make me someone else,
Nice dresses, shoes, T-shirts and hair.
I had enough of this
I'm only myself.

You want to make me somebody I'm not,
You even took away all the fun I had,
Don't think I'm a super man
Remember that I'm only myself.

I don't have super powers,
I don't know how to fly,
I don't know nothing amazing
I'm only me, myself because I am I.

Selena Siedlecka (12)
Mount Carmel RC Girls' School, London

What Goes Around Comes Around

A little girl alone in a room,
Not a sound,
Not a movement.
Suddenly the room is filled with loud voices,
A pack of ravenous vultures ready to pick on anyone less popular than them.
A loud sharp scream came to that room.
What goes around comes around, just as long as they're not bullying me!

A little knock on the door,
The sound of bones hitting the ground.
What goes around comes around, as long as they're not knocking on my door!

What goes around comes around!
What goes around comes around!
What goes around comes around you say!
The sound of heads clashing together
What goes around does come around.

Tiana Taleah Phyneasha James (11)
Mount Carmel RC Girls' School, London

Relationships

Will love help my soul to live?
Will love give me that freedom I never had?
Will love be that thing which makes me happy?
Love, love, love?

Will love be the answer to my worries?
Will love make my life happy by making a family?
Love, love, love?

Will love be there when I end my life to go to Heaven?
Will love be there when I go off to work?
Is love my world?

Nahima Choudhury (11)
Mount Carmel RC Girls' School, London

I Was Bad

I was bad
Very bad at every lesson
I had a lesson
I was bad
Very bad

They all laughed
At me
I did not care I carried on

I was bad
Very bad, very bad at every lesson
I had an exam
I was bad
Very bad

They teased
Me
I did not care, I carried on

I was bad
Very bad
I was the only girl with no friends
I only had one friend
They all punched
Me
I did not care, I carried on

I was bad
Very bad
I had a friend
She helps me
I was bad
Very bad

They all hated
Me
I did not care, I carried on

I was bad
Very bad at university
I was bad
Very bad

They all ran away from
Me
I did not care, I carried on

I had my final exam
I was good
Very good

They all like
Me
I really don't care what they say to me
All I think is to try your best.

Pelin Dogan (11)
Mount Carmel RC Girls' School, London

Why Me?

Why?
Why do I drink
And get drunk
Let the police come and take me away
To jail?
Why, why, why me?

Why?
Why do I kill and
Go to jail just because
Someone looked at me
For no reason?
Why, why, why me?

Why?
Why do I take drugs
To hurt myself
And take away all my pain?
Why, why, why me?

Why?
Why do I miss school
For senseless things
Then not graduate to uni?
Why, why, why me?

Why?
Why don't any of my jobs I apply for
Accept me, is it because of my rep?
Why, why, why me?

Why?
I wonder what my future will be like
I bet it will be terrible.

Why?
So now life's over for me
And there is no need to wonder about my future
Now no more
Why, why, why me?

Glorianna Famuyiwa-Kennedy (11)
Mount Carmel RC Girls' School, London

Not My Business

I look out the window
What do I see?
Crime, I see crime
But that's not my business.

I look out the window
What do I see?
Shooting a girl and her little brother too
But that's not my business.

I look out the window
What do I see?
A girl just answered her question to a sexual assault
But that's not my business.

I look out the window, what do I see?
Oh no, the boy's pointing at me.
He knocks and slams the door open
But it's too late,
I have no sight.

Georgia Higgins (11)
Mount Carmel RC Girls' School, London

Life

Life is hard
Life is what we have to live for
Life is what we need
What would we do without life?

In life there is family
Family is what we need in life
Life is yourself and life is you
We should love life
We need life to stay alive
What would you do if you did not have life?

Life is all about you living it
In life there is school, job, fashion and more things
Why do people have to live life?
They live life to get an injection and other things
Some people think life is great
Some people think life is bad
But what do you think of life?

Wendy Fozoo (12)
Mount Carmel RC Girls' School, London

Friends, Friends, Friends

Friends, friends, friends,
Can you trust them all these days?
Don't know what's gone into them
But these are just the days.

You either have loads or few
But which one's made for you
Have they ever bullied you
Or even made you feel blue?

So, pick your friends very wisely
'Cause the mistakes can be very pricey
(And if you go down the wrong route)
They could make your life a whole lot of pain
Drive you insane
So think again . . .

Joanna El Hajjar (12)
Mount Carmel RC Girls' School, London

Knives, Guns, Death

The darkened road, the frightful nights
My friends all say it will be alright.
Knives, guns, death.

Hoodies on, swaggering along,
Avoiding them all night long.
Knives, guns, death.

I stop to stare, the evil glare
All around me everywhere.
Knives, guns, death.

They beat me like clay, at night, not day
I want them all to go away.
Knives, guns, death.

The friends I'll miss, my family's kiss
This will be my final wish.

Chloe Barrow (12)
Mount Carmel RC Girls' School, London

I Love You

I love you so much
You don't know how happy I am when we touch
You have no clue how much I care
I even like the style of your hair
I love you

You didn't always feel the same
Yet each time I called you always came
Our relationship has been like a bumpy road
It's almost like we got our own secret code
I love you

I'd die happy spending the rest of my life with you
Hopefully you would too
Too bad
I'm sad
You're not here anymore
Maybe you'll show up on 'Jersey Shore'
Wherever you are I hope you're happy
And the girl you're with ain't too shabby
For you to be happy I would kill
I love you, always have and always will
I love you.

Chanda Chileshe (12)
Mount Carmel RC Girls' School, London

Should I Or Shouldn't I?

My friends are all doing it,
I've seen it on TV,
I know how they do it so,
Should I or shouldn't I?

They sniff crack,
I know it's not right,
But they all ask me to so,
Should I or shouldn't I?

Drugs are bad,
But they don't care,
They tell me it's fun so,
Should I or shouldn't I?

A 16-year-old dies,
A mother cries,
The heroin killed her,
Should I or shouldn't I?

I think to myself,
Do I want to die?
And make my mother cry?
No. Drugs are bad and I want to live a life.

Mehret Zelalem (12)
Mount Carmel RC Girls' School, London

Never Ending Tear Drops

He followed Ky home from school one day,
Chased him down a road that only went one way,
He screamed for help and tried to pull away,
Now Ky sleeps forever in peace,
Forever will his family cry.

He followed Yaz to the shop one day,
Threw her in a car and drove away,
He held a knife to her throat,
She tried to scream for help,
Now Yaz sleeps forever in peace,
Forever will her family cry.

I walk on my own to school every day,
I know I don't want to die in that way,
I don't want to scream in need of help,
I don't want to cry and scream and yelp,
I want to stay alive and die of old age,
Rest in peace for all the victims of a knife,
You didn't deserve to lose your life,
Forever will your family cry.

Chanelle Foskett (13)
Mount Carmel RC Girls' School, London

Bad Day

You wake up in the morning,
Look in the mirror.
It's gonna be a bad hair day today,
It looks as if there's a bush on your head,
It's gonna be a bad day today.

You look in the café window,
Someone stares right back.
Is that someone really you?
'Cause that someone's gaining weight
Chubby, plump, round 'n' fat
It's gonna be a bad day today.

You look in the clothes shop window
Stare at the new clothes.
Pretty things, but what a price!
Someone walks past and shouts,
'What ugly clothes you're wearing!'
It's gonna be a bad day today,
Just gonna have to grin and bear it.

Lauren Stafford (12)
Mount Carmel RC Girls' School, London

Always Boys

Walk the streets with a pocket full of drugs,
But they don't care because they're thugs.
Money, love, drugs and bling,
But being popular that's the main thing.

Stealing cars and making money,
But they don't care as long as they have a good looking honey.
They spit rhymes and buss raps thinking they're kings,
But being popular that's the main thing.

Snip, snap, prick and click the sound of handcuffs on their wrists,
But they don't care as long as they brag about the girl they kissed.
Their parents wait by the phone, waiting for it to ring, ring
But being popular that's the main thing!

Shannia Candice Carson (11)
Mount Carmel RC Girls' School, London

Why Can't I? It's Not Fair

If my friends are allowed
To drink what they want
Why can't I? It's not fair!

They bring it to school
I can't drink
I don't even know what
It tastes like, so why not?
My decision, why not?
It's not fair, why can't I?

My friends and I go shopping
She forces me to drink
I take it and start
I get addicted to it
I hate it but I want more
It's disgusting, why did I want it?

Hiremala Mesfun (11)
Mount Carmel RC Girls' School, London

It's Not My Business

They jump out from nowhere
The boys attack
The boy who is getting beaten
Didn't know what was behind his back
But it's not my business
I'm not gonna be the one who is like that.

The boy jumps out from behind her back
I know it's a sexual attack
She screams and kicks
But there is no escape for her
But it's not my business
I'm not gonna be the one who is like that.

She gets the questions right
They throw crunched up papers at her back
The water from her eyes is like a waterfall
She is my friend
But it's not my business
I'm not gonna be the one who is like that.

He puffs and puffs as the cigarette goes in and out of his mouth
He drinks and gulps every sip of vodka, I know what he is doing to his body
It's not good for him, I can stop him but it's not my business
I'm not gonna be the one who is like that.

I see her putting up the rope adjusting the height
She's in my college and I know that her parents have been fighting
She puts her neck in the rope hole and pulls it tight
Then she starts to lose sight.
Her eyes are closed, she's dead
But it's not my business
I'm not gonna be the one who is like that.

I'm sat on the bench; I see a girl jump for joy
Her grades are high, they are all celebrating
But now it's my turn, I'm being chased
It is now my business.

Whitney Ikenwe (11)
Mount Carmel RC Girls' School, London

On The Streets Of London

Andrew carries a knife all the time
But on the streets of London there is always a lie.
They say it's for protection, but is it just that?
But on the streets in London there's always a knife.

He's one with the knife, but fights for his life.
He shows it to his friends but one policeman walks by
But does nothing, but why?
But on the streets of London there's always someone in the wrong.

A child walks by, a bunch full of boys
Then gets pulled aside by one of the boys
I think it's a sexual assault but I am not sure
But what problem of mine is it if I am not involved?
He pulls out a knife and shows it to the child!
The child runs off home.
But on the streets of London there's always one scared child.

As I get on the bus I get shooed and pulled
But upstairs on the bus he sits near me.
He pulls me by the hair then shoves it in me.
I cough and cough as blood pours out my mouth
But on the streets of London no one heard my shout.

Natalie Kyereme (11)
Mount Carmel RC Girls' School, London

Relationship

That boy over there
He's watching, he's watching that girl.
She's dancing, dancing and singing.
But that boy over there,
Why is he watching, what is he waiting for?
The girl has finished, finished her song,
She has got to go home.
The boy, where did he go?
The girl is waiting, it's late it's . . .
The boy there, he's there.
He's watching, he sees the bus but . . .
That girl she's gone and never to be seen.
Her mum weeping at her dead daughter's grave,
How did she die?
I'll give you one guess, that boy,
That boy behind the curtain,
The boy at the bus stop,
He was the one watching and waiting.
The boy was the one who brought this pain.

Megan Stuart (11)
Mount Carmel RC Girls' School, London

I Don't Care What Happens (Knife Crime)

Last night I saw three young people
With blood on their hands and shirts
Rushing up the street was police cars.
I don't care what happens.

I heard somebody is in hospital from a stab wound
I think it was from the night before.
I don't care what happens.

Outside I heard somebody screaming for help
Then heard, 'Run bro, run, before they come.'
I don't care what happens.

Last night I was the one who got stabbed
I was the one crying for help
Police rushing up the street
I was in the hospital
But who will care about me?

Louise Lau (12)
Mount Carmel RC Girls' School, London

Am I Bothered?

I walk down the street
I look at my peeps
I see something sharp from under their sleeves
They look back at me
Am I bothered?

Some next up boy
Passes by us
We surround him
He takes a knife out
My peeps take one too
But . . .
Am I bothered?

I can see, now right through
His young boy chest
I scream,
I shout,
I die too
But is anyone bothered?

Angelika Wroblewska (12)
Mount Carmel RC Girls' School, London

Don't Come Near Me Coz I Got A Shank

I carry it coz I want some respect
If you don't have a knife they will call you a sket.
I don't like my mum, I don't like my dad,
All they yabba yabba is, 'You're so bad!'
I said, 'Don't come near me coz I got a shank.'

My sister thinks I'm crazy
Coz my girlfriend's expecting a baby.
I said, 'You must be mad
Do you really think I wanna be a dad?'
I said, 'Don't come near me coz I got a shank.'

I don't want a baby
Hell yeah, I might be crazy.
God I don't know what to do
So I chose to turn to you
But all I say is, 'Don't come near me coz I got a shank.'

I couldn't take it anymore
My life was a mess.
Guess what happened, just guess, guess, guess?
I took my shank and stuck it in my heart
I screamed, 'Ouch, oww, bloodart!'
Don't worry because now I'm at peace
Now all of you can celebrate with a really big feast!

Shameika Precious Tello-Smith (13)
Mount Carmel RC Girls' School, London

I Will Only Achieve This If . . .

In the future,
I want to be a doctor,
I want to save people's lives,
I want to help people when they're unwell,
I will only achieve this if I try my best.

In the future,
I want to be a teacher,
Looking smart and feeling smart,
Helping people with their studies when they don't understand,
I will only achieve this if I try my best.

In the future,
I want to be a dentist,
I want to drill people's teeth,
I want people to have strong and healthy teeth,
I will only achieve this if I try my best.

In the future,
I want to be anything I want to be,
And I can only achieve this if I try my best.

Tasnim Chowdhury (11)
Mount Carmel RC Girls' School, London

Open Doors

Me, myself and I,
Primary school was full of wonders,
Big Ben, telling me it's time to leave,
Ding dong!
Open the door, close the door,
I am so confused.

Leaving my friends,
Seeing new people,
Looking around,
Am I being the new trend?
Open the door, close the door,
I am so confused.

Am I looking cool?
That was a rhetorical question,
Or just being a fool,
Trying to walk with swagger,
Open the door, close the door,
I am so confused.

Now my future changes,
I hear the clanging chimes of doom.
Secondary school scares me off my feet,
I walk through that door!
Open the door, close the door,
I am so confused.

My eyes gleaming but
Remembering the first time,
I was scared going to nursery, crying,
Open the door, close the door,
I am so confused.

Feeling like I am the one man,
Standing for my school,
Like I'm in a different whole new world.
Open the door, close the door,
I am so confused.

Having new friends,
With a smile,
Open the door, close the door,
I know where I'm going.

Doyin Ajiboye (11)
Mount Carmel RC Girls' School, London

It's Not Just Me!

I was at a party with my friends
We were gathered round a table
Packets of it laid in the table . . . it was drugs!
They were all taking it not just me
Putting it down their throats like candy

They were all teasing me, they said I had to
I knew I had to if they were to accept me
They were all taking it, not just me
Putting it down their throats like candy

I got addicted; I started to deal it for money
They were all taking it, not just me
Putting down their throats like candy

I went to court, to jail then rehab to try and get clean
My so-called friends got away with the bad deed
They were all taking it, not just me
Putting down their throats like candy

But now I'm clean, clean as can be
But then you'll see more shall start taking it
Then you'll see it wasn't just me
More shall start to put it down their throats like candy.

Lashai Modest-Norville (12)
Mount Carmel RC Girls' School, London

Future

The future holds untold secrets
Waiting to be discovered
Mysterious and wonderful
The future is the beginning

Technology improves
Day by day
What does the future have to bring?
The future is the beginning

What will happen?
Nobody knows
As years go past
The future is the beginning

As you can see
You cannot tell what will happen
Boom!
What just happened?

Ihuoma Anyanwu (11)
Mount Carmel RC Girls' School, London

Future

The big business
People walking
Along on the phone
Will I have a future
Be known in a
Career?

The fashions lying
Around everywhere,
One blink, open
Your eyes and there
It lies.
Will I have a future
Designing an object
That people would
Use?

The books that
People read and
Take ideas to help
Them. Will I have a
Future writing so
People can read and
Learn?

You hear the radio
And their great
Voices,
Will I have a future
Singing people
Listening to my
Voice?

You see the doctors
Doing extraordinary
Things, saving
People's lives,
Will I have a future
Saving people who
Need help?

You can see or read
The amazing things
Lawyers do to get
People out of justice.
Will I have a future
Helping people get
Out of trouble?

I should think, will I
Have a future? Have
A family, a career,
Will I have a
Life?

Carina Abrue (11)
Mount Carmel RC Girls' School, London

Music

Life grabs it by the neck
Strangling it till it falls.
My broken heart,
My broken music note.

He unwinds the tape
And wraps it around my bleeding soul.
My broken heart,
My broken music note.

Blood trickles onto the damp floor
As the CD plays on.
My broken heart,
My broken music note.

They stab me in the back
As the melody drifts away.
My broken heart,
My broken music note.

The screams ring in my ear
Of the drowning girl.
My broken heart,
My broken music note.

It takes me back to my day
Of my broken heart,
And of my broken music note.

Nada Alkhafaji (11)
Mount Carmel RC Girls' School, London

My Mother

This pain of mine is growing . . .

When I think back to the times I spent with you . . .
My heart urges for some kind of relief, some kind of comfort,
A comfort which may release all this pain and suffering.
You were the one who taught me about life,
You were the one who made me who I am today,
Yet these miles that lie between us are separating our love,
Are separating us from being the same.

The reason it hurts is because our souls are connected;
Maybe they always have been and will be.
Maybe we've lived a thousand lives and in each one we were forced apart, apart for the same reason.

This distance that keeps us from being together may be far,
But love doesn't count miles it is measured by the heart.

Oh Mother, if only I could see your smile
If only once Mother, once you could appear in front of me
And hold me like a mother holds her baby.
Keep me warm, because I have never been in a position like that since dawn.

When I imagine you, I see your beauty and grace,
And know that they have grown stronger in every dream that I have dreamt about you.

I have spent every dream looking for you,
Not someone like you . . . but you.
Mother please, tell me, tell me - why have we been forced apart?
Why us, why?

This pain is growing of mine . . .

I shall continue dear mother to search,
But just, just if I don't meet you again and this is truly goodbye,

I know that I will see you in another dream, my mother . . .

Zohra Dost Mohammad (13)
Paddington Academy, London

Living The Dream

I'm going to be the next big star.
I'm going to be the best and better than the rest.
I'm going to win all the awards.
I'm going to be on the front of every magazine.
I'm going to be LA's favourite.
I'm going to be everything you want.
I'm going to have the nicest car around.
I'm going to be the richest person around.
I'm going to be the first person ever to be a star.
I'm going to have the biggest house around.
I'm going to buy LA and Miami.
I'm going to be everything,
This is what I want to be!

Elliot Brace (12)
Pontarddulais Comprehensive School, Swansea

Love

Love,
A razor to the soul,
Eternal bleeding spilling
Outside, like walking
On broken glass. Love,
Someone you miss burning
A hole inside.
A dagger in the soul,
Sinking deeper and deeper.

Holly Archer (13)
Pontarddulais Comprehensive School, Swansea

Summer

Summer is warm,
Summer is cool,
Tanned and brown
All ready for school.

Bikes and beaches
Surfboard and boat
Ready to paddle
Ready afloat.

Waking up to sun,
Waking up to fun,
I'm up and alert
Then laughing till it hurts!

Excellent, exciting and the best
Magical, mystical, it's the greatest
Coats and gloves are coming out
My summer's over, what's yours about?

Molly Davies (12)
Pontarddulais Comprehensive School, Swansea

Anticipation

Anticipation,
A sea of nerves.
Anticipation,
A roller coaster on repeat.
Anticipation,
A fluttering butterfly
In your stomach.
Anticipation,
A ticking bomb.
Anticipation,
A rumble of your belly.
Anticipation
The tremble of fear.
Anticipation.

Liam Oak (13)
Pontarddulais Comprehensive School, Swansea

What's Important To Me?

My hamster
Is a gangster
When I give him cheese
I can tell that he'd say please
When he's in his ball
He loves to roll and roll
The good thing for his age
Is that he runs around his cage
When he falls asleep
I love to have a peep
And that is what's important to me!

I love you Milky.

Charlie Clarke (12)
Robert Bloomfield Middle School, Shefford

Freedom

Being free is the best
Doing what you want whenever you want
It's great fun
Some people don't have freedom
Those who do
Take it for granted
As a child
I love it
I take it for granted
Should I?
Should anyone?
Everyone loves it
Everyone wants it
Freedom lets you
Go where you want
Do what you want
I'm lucky
To have freedom
It's better now
Most people have it
But
Not everyone
It's unfair
It's not their fault
It's not my fault.

Sophie Tate (13)
Robert Bloomfield Middle School, Shefford

Life And Death

Life, I don't see it anymore,
I'm in the grips of death,
I see life now. Glowing, beautiful, shining life,
I see them now. Fighting life and death,
I'm thrown to one side,
Thinking who will win?
My life's restored,
Everything's back to how it was,
Life must have won!
Otherwise Death would have me,
Forever more.

Kayleigh Jupp (12)
Robert Bloomfield Middle School, Shefford

That's My Mutt!

I have a dog that's soft and white
If you annoy him he tends to bite
He welcomes me home every night
But sometimes gives me a terrible fright!

I have a dog that chases bees
He gives me love, we have memories
We play outside underneath the trees
Sometimes he barks and catches fleas!

I have a dog that's really small
He throws his toys against the wall
We all wish that he was tall
Then none of us would ever fall!

Olivia Hitchen (13)
Robert Bloomfield Middle School, Shefford

The Things That Matter To Me

The things that matter to me?
Well, let me see . . .

Little kids with smiling faces,
World peace from all the places.
I hate it when people squish bugs,
One thing I love will always be hugs.
Singing and clothes, I will always enjoy,
Though to be completely honest I am pretty coy.

The things I see, you won't,
I don't care that you don't.

See the birds from far away,
Going on holiday.
Chocolate at some point will take over the world,
I love my hair, especially when it's curled.
Leaf ants will one day build our house,
I really want a pet mouse.

Poaching should stop, now, today,
Fur coats and rugs should be banned right away.

Reggae music will come back in fashion,
The colours of the rainbow will represent passion.
My dog, Duma, I could never let go,
Duma means pride in Polish you know.
Art, I find, relaxes my mind,
You're not a friend if you're not kind.

Only a few things left to say,
Bonjour, buenos dias, dzień dobry and good day.

Lauren Wylot (12)
Robert Bloomfield Middle School, Shefford

Zzzzz . . .

My bed, my bed, my brilliant bed
The perfect place to rest my head
A place to sleep, a place to dream
Or a nightmare if I'm feeling mean.

But how is my bed one of the best?
You have to try it, give it a test
It's warm and cosy, just like a nest
And when I wake up, I'm full of zest.

My bed, my bed, my brilliant bed
It matters to me and that's all can be said!

Katie Summerfield (13)
Robert Bloomfield Middle School, Shefford

Ode To An iPod

The room goes boom when I'm in with a thump,
When I'm on iPod playing Doodle Jump!
While I'm waiting for an update I'll be on Facebook,
Or reading the latest Harry Potter on iBook.
My iPod is a stunner, a runner, although it can't fly,
The speakers are loud (5 watts isn't shy!)
There's an app for this and there's an app for that,
So much you can fit into something small and flat!
A razzle and a dazzle in the room I go,
You'll be bugging for a turn, friend or foe.
Stereo, TV, books, App Store,
I'll tell you one thing, there's only more.
There is so much to do, am I spoilt for choice?
Now the sounds gone, I can only hear my voice!
The battery is low, what should I do?
I lost my charger, I think I'm doomed!

Ryan Coxall (13)
Robert Bloomfield Middle School, Shefford

Snowflakes

Snowflakes are high when they fall from the sky
None are the same, you calling me insane?
Just need you to know that I really like snow
But when they melt, my heart melts too
Just so you know, I love my snow.

Ryan Donohoe (12)
Robert Bloomfield Middle School, Shefford

My Furry Friend

My rabbit Daisy is black with white paws.
She is friendly but has very sharp claws.
Her ears are small and neat,
She also has very large back feet.

She hops around the garden at night
Until next door's cat gives her a fright.
Her nose does constantly twitch,
But oh her fur does make me itch.

In the garden she loves to dig
Holes that are monstrously big.
One large hole my sister fell down
And she came up all muddy and brown.

At the end of the day when it's time for bed
She runs away and hides in the shed.
Although she drives me round the bend,
She'll always be my best friend.

Emily Ashwin (12)
Robert Bloomfield Middle School, Shefford

It's Made From A Tree

I rest my head
Upon my bed
When my eyes are as heavy as lead!

My bed is the best
It's bigger and more comfy than the rest.
I'll let you give it a try
But it's not for you to buy!

I go to bed
To get my rest
So I look my very best!

My bed's not hard
But it's thicker than card.
It's made from a tree
And it's just for me!

Laura Warren (13)
Robert Bloomfield Middle School, Shefford

Books, Books! Brilliant Books

Books, books, where do you start?
Fiction, fantasy or books about art?
Personally I like fantasy
But that isn't some people's cup of tea
Some prefer action, horror, adventure and humour
And I prefer a right old boomer.

A book must be gripping, absorbing, consuming,
I just can't continue if it isn't moving.
I love the way the pages turn
With every look I continue to learn.
Books, books, where would I be
Without them there to help guide me?

Charlotte Buckingham (13)
Robert Bloomfield Middle School, Shefford

I Love To Dance

Dance, dance to the music
Dance, dance to the beat
Dance, dance with the competitors
While dancing to compete.

I dance for laughter
I dance for tears
I dance for friendship
So come on let's cheer
I dance for hopes
I create the dreams.

I dance for the love
I dance even when I feel pain
I dance knowing there is something to gain
I dance for love
I dance for me
I dance for everyone to see.

Sophie Dear (11)
Robert Bloomfield Middle School, Shefford

Contemporary

It ain't street
It ain't jazz
You don't do it with the lads
It ain't fast but it ain't slow
Okay, really here we go
So are you ready
For the show
Of your lifetime
The curtains open and you'll hear the chimes
Have you guessed it?
It's contemporary time!

Charlie Maxwell (11)
Robert Bloomfield Middle School, Shefford

What Matters To Me?

What matters to me?
Flowers and curls,
Being free,
Dresses and swirls,
Happiness is the key,
What matters to me?

What matters to me?
Friends near and far,
Family and their tree,
People who don't go, 'Ha, ha, ha, ha,'
Believing in me,
What matters to me?

What matters to me?
Animals big and small,
The wind in my hair as I fly down the field,
On a quad bike that's fast,
Things that are real,
What matters to me?

What matters to me?
Having a mind of my own, being able to think,
Not being thrown around like I'm not alive,
Feeling important,
Feeling loved,
What matters to me?

What matters to me?
Being different,
Books that make you think and are realistic,
People who are quiet, but ballistic,
Having a personality that isn't mean and stale,
What matters to me?

What matters to me?
Not being a bully,
Being accepted,
What other people think of me,
Being early and not late,
What matters to me?

What matters to me?
Respect,
Dreams,
People who have good humour,
Old cottages with beams,
What matters to me?

What matters to me?
Being helpful, being kind,
What friends say,
Being me,
Not being a fake,
What matters to me?

What matters to me?
Running around,
Hockey,
Coming back from holiday, homeward bound,
Being in the rain, getting wet,
What matters to me?

What matters to me?
Won't matter to you,
Won't matter to most people,
What matters most to me,
Is being true,
These things matter to me.
What matters to you?

Lucie Baker (12)
Robert Bloomfield Middle School, Shefford

What Matters To Me?

What matters to me is my art, my friends and family,
The reliability,
The creativity
And the activity.
The faith,
The truth,
The hope and peace,
Not the lies,
The wars,
The fights,
The scores.

What matters to me is my art, my friends and family.
What matters to me ain't what matters to you,
It's different.
It's what makes me, me, not me, you.

What matters to me is my art, my friends and family.
The happiness
And my creativity.
My future,
The sky
Flying high,
Soaring by,
Goodbye
And that's what matters to me, can't you see?

Dionne Gray (13)
Robert Bloomfield Middle School, Shefford

What Matters To Me?

What matters to me,
Is running through the sea,
Being free,
That's what matters to me.

The freedom of speech,
Eating a peach,
Or looking at bleach,
That's what matters to me.

What matters to me,
Are the people I meet,
The people I greet,
That's what matters to me.

People I see in movies,
Watch on TV,
Listen on my iPod,
That's who I want to be.

Justin Bieber,
Taylor L,
Or Robert P,
They're who I want to be.

What matters to me,
Is making a difference.

Rachel Silverwood (12)
Robert Bloomfield Middle School, Shefford

Nature Poem

As I sit on the grass,
Looking up at the sky,
I watch as the clouds float happily by.
When I lay in my bed,
Gazing at the beautiful stars,
I think about how lucky I am to be here.
At the beach,
I rest on the sand listening to the waves viciously crash.
When the seagulls loudly gabble and gossip,
I think about how lucky I am to be here.
To be out in the open air,
As it whooshes past my ears,
And to smell the fresh scent of flowers and grass,
I think about how lucky I am to be here.
As I sit here and wonder what other great sights there are to see,
I make sure I am grateful and here I am lucky to be.

Corrie Puleston (13)
Robert Bloomfield Middle School, Shefford

My Dog

I have a dog called Kade
He really has it made.
He's my best dog
But he runs like a demented frog.

When we go to the park
He likes to run and bark.
When he sees a cat
He lays down like a mat.

But when we play
I wouldn't have it any other way.
My dog makes me proud
But I wish he was as light as a cloud.

Cameron Mitchell (11)
Robert Bloomfield Middle School, Shefford

My Xbox 360

What matters to me is my Xbox 360
I am an Xbox-aholic you can't stop me
When I saw that box under the Christmas tree
I could not wait to go and see
But my mum said I had to eat my tea.
I ate my dinner not leaving a pea
So I could go and play my Xbox 360.

Finley Chapman (11)
Robert Bloomfield Middle School, Shefford

A Girl Who Cries A Thousand Broken Hearts

When Vans, South Poles and Converses hit the floor
It's as if someone's smashing a door.
Love is evil, love is poison, love is blind,
Those are words that spring to mind.

Smudged mascara down her cheek
Her eyes are blurry, her emotions are weak.
Break my heart, you make me smile,
It's been broken for a long, long while.

Pouring rain outside her door,
A thousand teardrops on the floor.
Even though there's a million messages on her phone
She's still feeling so, so alone.

She locks her door,
She lies on the floor,
Grabs her notebook and starts to cry,
Crosses out the hearts she'd drawn and asks herself why.

How could I've been so blind?
All he did was play with my mind.
There's more important things than having a husband or a wife
Like you know, living your life!

Bethany Kay (11)
Robert Bloomfield Middle School, Shefford

Friends

Everyone needs someone
No matter where they come from
It's not fair to be left out
This is what I want to talk about.

Not everyone has the chance
To meet someone on first glance
Who is kind, funny and a star
Just like the way you are.

Friends are always on my mind
Because they are all so very kind.
I don't know what I would do
If friends were not with you.

Well, that's what means a lot to me
Friends that I want to be.
Don't be alone, be with a mate
Or you will be in such a state.

Ella Ofstedahl (13)
Robert Bloomfield Middle School, Shefford

A Dragon's Heart

Diving, soaring through the skies,
Ruby, glowing, bright red eyes.
Shimmering scales of every colour,
Each one different to any other.
A breath of flame fills the air,
But really of course they do care.
A dragon's heart is as true as it says,
A companion and friend for many days.

Lucy Fredrickson (12)
Robert Bloomfield Middle School, Shefford

Forgotten Wonders

Have you seen that golden trophy,
With its unique brown chest?
That small blacky-red head
With its smudged white breast?

What about the robin,
With its deep brown eyes?
Its gorgeous red chest -
Eating all those pesky flies?

Have you seen that spooky ghost,
Flying silently overhead?
With a great big mouse hanging from its beak
Scaring you in bed?

Birds are forgotten wonders . . .
Special animals
Hiding in thick woodland
Grassland, lakes or trees.

Joshua Rayner (12)
Robert Bloomfield Middle School, Shefford

Chocolate

Chocolate is delicious
Chocolate is mysterious
It sometimes goes crack
Like a KitKat
You can smell it with your nose
It is pretty like a rose
It sometimes can be white
I could eat it all night
The chocolate goes crack
After that I need a nap.

Millie Ramsay Waite (11)
Robert Bloomfield Middle School, Shefford

Anti-Racism

Black or white
Rich or poor
Why must these
Be reasons for war?
We are all one
At least we should be!
We are all equal
So why can't you see?
We should all trust one another
We should all be friends
Because this really isn't how
Our planet should end.
Anti-racism means a lot to me
No one should be treated so bad
Knowing how cruel some people are
Why does this not make you sad?
Everyone in this world deserves
To be treated right
So let's step out of the darkness
And let's switch on the light.

Kyah Rooney (13)
Robert Bloomfield Middle School, Shefford

What Matters To Me

She jumps on my bed,
Squishing my head,
Squeezing me against the wall,
Like a ball,
Which I am not at all.

Constantly moving,
Leaving me fuming,
Nonstop teasing,
Biting and squeezing,
Till everyone screams.

On and off my mum and dad's bed,
Doing Dad's head,
Mum just laughs,
I just giggle,
She is such a pickle.

Always ready to play,
This is all day,
Part of the gang,
Only with fangs,
Pain in the bum,
But always good fun.

Tall and fluffy,
Skinny and scruffy,
My dog Willow.

Ryan White (12)
Robert Bloomfield Middle School, Shefford

Sprint

Like a statue, I stand in line,
Only one thing on my mind . . .

The crack in the air as the gun is fired,
My heart's racing, but I'm not even tired.

Some drop behind, others thrive,
I push off my feet and start to drive.

Pushing to the limit, winning but wait . . .

A single beat coming from behind,
No it can't be, it's just in my mind.

I have to drop back or just fight the pain,
And the thunder of feet comes back again.

Now I'm scared, I'm coming last,
The time is going really fast.

I only seem to have one choice,
'You've got to win!' said my inner voice.

My last energy reserve, the final push,
And then out of nowhere a sudden whoosh!

I'm leading again, I'm finally there,
It's so close, I cannot bear.

A judge walks over and says, 'You're first!'
And there's me thinking I was the worst!

Gregory Hill (12)
Robert Bloomfield Middle School, Shefford

My Bass Guitar

When my guitar
Makes me a star,
I'm going to buy me
A big ass car.

When my guitar
Takes me far
I am going to drink
Jack Daniels in
Every bar.

When I rock out
With my guitar
I am going to make
Me and my band
Go far.

When I make it
With my guitar
I am going to be
A righteous raving
Rock 'n' roll star.

Adam Buckingham (12)
Robert Bloomfield Middle School, Shefford

What Matters To Me

What matters to me might not matter to you
But that's not the point now is it.
What matters to me is culture,
To embrace the spirit, the music, the art.

The sound of music passing by
Like the milkman at your doorstep.
Music is a wonderful thing
But can music be wonderful if there is no one to hear it?

I wish, just one wish
That can only be understood through the heart of an artist.
I wish that art would come alive, leap out of the paper
And it would greet you, meet you and complete you.

I don't know what I'd do without it,
What we'd do without it.
It's not an opinion.
It's not a statement.
It's a fact.
If culture didn't exist then all the creative things would just vanish.
No sport, no music, no art, no nothing would exist without culture.

Harvey Lake (12)
Robert Bloomfield Middle School, Shefford

What Matters To Me

What matters to me,
What matters to me,
A lot of things matter to me,
But one thing that does,
Is becoming famous!

Becoming famous would be amazing,
Walking down the bright red carpet,
News reports and cameras flashing,
My face in magazines, that would be smashing!

Going to a club,
All night long,
Getting in newspapers,
For things I've done wrong!

All of the money,
That I would earn,
My life's like a party,
It's only just started!

James Hitchen (13)
Robert Bloomfield Middle School, Shefford

Shooting Star Car

What matters to me are fast cars
That zoom about like a shooting star
So when I'm older I really should
Get a nice car if I could!

My favourite car's a Pagani Zonda
That zooms about with blind and wonder.
So when I'm out in the street
I see the people on their feet.

Saying, 'I wish I was in that car,
Zooming about like a shooting star!
With a big house and lots of money
Who lived in the country, nice and sunny!'

I saw a car that looked so old
It looked so damaged, it looked so cold
And I thought of how lucky I can be,
How this car's so fast, it sets me free!

Harvey Peirson (12)
Robert Bloomfield Middle School, Shefford

Rugby

I love to play rugby,
You get all wet and grubby,
My mum has a fit,
When she sees the state of my kit,
Mud on the sleeves,
And dirt on my knees.

When I play the game,
Scoring tries is my aim,
Kicking penalties,
Is not one of my specialties,
But rucking and mauling,
I can do that all morning.

When I am on the pitch,
There is a personality switch,
I leave my manners behind,
As I lose my mind,
No smiling and grinning,
All I care about is winning.

When the final whistle goes,
There are no more blows,
Handshakes all around,
And I buy the first round,
We are the winning team,
What a game it's been!

Lewis McCracken (13)
Robert Bloomfield Middle School, Shefford

Flash

What matters to me is my dog, Flash,
He's always on the move and loves to dash.
He is completely awesome and fun,
If we had a race, he'd be crowned number one.

Flash is the best, trust me I know,
He especially loves the white winter snow.
His eyes are the best; they are big and bright,
He always uses them in the night.

When Flash is happy he always barks
That's only because he loves the dark.
He has a white patch on his chest,
I obviously know that he is the best.

Kelsey Newlin (11)
Robert Bloomfield Middle School, Shefford

Animal Cruelty

If I was an animal, just for a day,
I wouldn't be the murderer – I'd be the prey,
Cooped up in a cage, screaming with rage,
Just spare a thought for us, hey?

Everywhere you look there are traces of us,
Spare a moment; you'll see why we're fussed,
Poor battery hens and rabbits in pens,
All we want is to earn your trust.

Testing medicine, make-up, shampoo,
Being your slaves is all that we do,
Providing cheap eggs, we can't move our legs,
But you don't really care, do you?

Leyla Ghaemi (11)
Robert Bloomfield Middle School, Shefford

Snowflakes

Fall for miles from the sky,
Under microscope stunning to the eye.
Never identical, so very unique,
In your hand they will melt in a blink.
So many different sizes,
The beauty always surprises.

Delicate like lace, so cold, touching my face.
I wish I could take some flakes home with me,
To share their beauty for all to see!
If flakes were to come on Christmas day,
It would mean more to me that words could say.
When springtime is here it's never the same,
Too long to wait for snowflakes again!

Amy Hannan (11)
Robert Bloomfield Middle School, Shefford

Friends

Friends are great, they make me smile
They keep their promise and that's worth a mile!

Each day we get together to have lots of fun,
We play about; it's always nicer in the sun.
We have sleepovers and tell jokes
But we always end up waking the old folks!

When we eventually sleep they don't hear a peep,
Until the morning at the crack of dawn we all get dressed with a yawn.

'Breakfast is ready,' Mum would shout, we would go down while Dad's not about.
We would eat and drink and have a think of what to do today,
I know, I thought, 'Mum, can my friends stay?'

Megan Sizer (11)
Robert Bloomfield Middle School, Shefford

Friendship

Friends are always there for you,
When you are down they always know what to do,
Perhaps a friend is like a ghost,
Their spirit never dies.
Nothing can beat the joy of friendship,
Not even money, jewellery or pies.
Life gives us many different things, good and bad, happy or sad,
But one of the best gifts we get is the love of a good friend.
Having a truly good friend means that if you are falling or failing in any sort of way,
You know that someone will always be there to catch you,
They are your friend,
And they are here to stay.
Friendship is not a laughing matter,
As you know that someone is there for you,
Waiting to catch you,
Right to the end.
A special person helps the road seem straighter,
And helps you get round every bend,
They make each day seem greater,
That special person is your loving friend.
You may sometimes find yourself asking,
Where would the world be if we didn't have any friends.

Brittany Mooney (11)
Robert Bloomfield Middle School, Shefford

Things I Like And Are Important

I love being good at reading
Books in the library which I am seeing
Buying their books that I am keeping
Heaping on the bedside window
Nature, fiction, non-fiction
I think I am having an addiction
And how could I forget about dictionaries?
I go to the Post Office to buy a comic
Especially the adventures of Wallace and Gromit
And there are other things that I like
Also a game called Bop It!
Computer games are fun
I can't wait until I'm done
I love the games that have guns
In-between I have a chocolate bar!
The important thing to me is school
I think it is a lot of fun
But I'm worried about getting this test wrong
So I have to finish before the bell goes ding dong!
My favourite lesson is PE
It's about being the best of my ability
But if I do not try my best . . .
I'm going to get a spanking!

Max Potter (11)
Robert Bloomfield Middle School, Shefford

Friends!

Friends matter to us,
Our friends make us laugh,
They guide us down the right path.

They support us whenever we're down,
Our caring friends,
They're always around.

We trust our friends,
No matter what,
They make us smile a lot.

Our friends are loyal,
They never doubt us,
They treat us like we are royal.

We love our friends,
Today and forever,
Ashleigh, Antonia, Lauren, Ellen, Rachel and Molly.

Friends matter to us,
Our friends make us laugh,
They guide us down the right path.

Antonia Nannetti (11) & Ellen Musgrove (12)
Robert Bloomfield Middle School, Shefford

Snow

Snow is white
Snow is pure
Snow is everything that means to me
As the snow falls slowly
I stick out my tongue
Every second the snow melts one by one until
The snow stops falling
My tongue feels fresh
I run to the field
I pick up some snow and
Start to build my marvellous
Snowman.
Once I've finished
Give it a name
Say goodbye.
I go home for tea
Always thinking of my
One and only best
Friend.
The snowman.

Georgia Pickett (11)
Robert Bloomfield Middle School, Shefford

What Matters To Me?

This is about things that matter to me,
It tells you why I want to belong, to be.
I like lots of things but sports the best,
I'm telling them to you to get them off my chest.

Trampolining is one of those things,
I like to jump, to bounce, to spring.
Front flips, I like to do,
Spinning round and round when I want to.

Guides is also very good,
Playing games and learning things we should.
Also making lots of friends,
And finding stuff to do, at dead ends.

Netball is kind of cool,
Shooting, passing, running with the ball.
Hoping to win the game,
All together and all the same.

Running really rules my life,
Striding, breathing, finding goals to strive.
Time trials, going fast,
Beating records and running past.

Dancing is the coolest ever,
Pliés, jazz fourths, are forever.
Modern, ballet, disco and street,
Dancing on to any beat.

Swimming is amazing too,
Front crawl, backstroke, breaststroke you do.
Getting wet and having fun,
Or swimming outside in the sun.

Orienteering is a perfect sport,
Finding checkpoints like you ought.
Ticking things off and running around,
In the woods and on rough ground.

The flute is a musical hobby,
I practise at school and in the lobby.
I blow so hard and play my notes,
Learn new tunes, like Mice and Boats.

Next up is my family and friends,
They are special right to the end.
I like playing with my friends at school,
My mum and dad and bro are cool.

This brings my poem to an end,
Hope you like it, tell your friends.
I made this about things that matter to me,
Now you have read it, now you can see.

Jessica Badgery (11)
Robert Bloomfield Middle School, Shefford

Black Socks

I love wearing my black socks.
I keep them in my special box.
I bring my socks to school,
And my friends think they are cool!

Every time I wear my crocks,
They look good with my socks.
Everyone seems to mock.
But when I wear them with my socks . . .
I can run like a fox.

When I go to bed at night,
I lie awake in a fright,
In case my black socks wash up white . . .
What a terrible sight!

Zak Jest (11)
Robert Bloomfield Middle School, Shefford

What You've Done To Me

Foundation revealing the real skin
A lot more tissues in the bin
Smudged mascara down your face
Now you walk in a slow pace
Broken heart you may now have
But don't let him have the last laugh.
You'll get him back but just be quick
He'll have a girlfriend before you know it
You're probably confused
But just don't show it
I need to get over you
But I can't because I need you
So my friends help me along
And say,
'Get over him . . . he may have ruined your mascara
But don't let him ruin your day!'

Madeline Symonds (12)
Robert Bloomfield Middle School, Shefford

What Matters To Me

What matters to me
Is the soldiers out there
Fighting for us
In the nightmare.

What matters to me
Is the men and the women
In camouflaged colours
While the trouble is brewing.

What matters to me
Is the courageous soldiers
Learning the tactics
And breaking the boulders.

What matters to me
Is my Dad and his friends
Fighting out there
Until the war ends.

Holly Smith (11)
Robert Bloomfield Middle School, Shefford

Autumn Harvest

Scarecrows standing in the fields,
With their button eyes,
Their carrot noses,
And the pumpkins growing
To make tasty pies.

The beautiful leaves falling off the trees ,
and the smell of a bonfire,
Next comes a creaking,
Of the old tractor tyre.

Soon will come the carving,
Carving a scary face,
On the pumpkin it will be,
Making trick or treat children race.

At 6 o'clock I look up,
Up at the great orange sky,
And once again another autumn day
Has sadly gone by.

Amber Bailey (11)
Robert Bloomfield Middle School, Shefford

Art

I'm quick and I'm patient,
I get the job done.

I'm neat and I'm careful,
Whilst having lots of fun.

I'm cheerful, I'm precise
I'm colourful
and on time.

Art travels with me throughout my life,
Along the bumpy roads I take
That I can't manage myself.

Art is like a mirror in my life,
I can see every step that I take and regret.

I trip, I fall,
I get back up and forget about it all.

Olivia Sandhu (11)
Robert Bloomfield Middle School, Shefford

Family

Family is most important to me
If it wasn't for them, I would not be!

First, there are my mum and dad
They're the best parents I ever had.

Then there's my brother – who can be annoying
And is always interfering to stop me enjoying.

Two nannies, two grandads at the top of the tree,
All four of them are special to me.

Jazzie, our dog, also lives with us
And she loves it when we make a fuss.

Do you want to hear more
Of my family galore?

The number of cousins I have is ten
I'm sure there'll be another one . . . wonder when!

Aunties and uncles in different shapes and sizes,
If there were competitions for the best, they'd win all the prizes.

See . . . family is most important to me!

Cameron Burgess (11)
Robert Bloomfield Middle School, Shefford

The Beautiful Game

Sunday morning
Game on.
Put on my kit
I'm feeling fit.

On the pitch,
We've seen the opposition,
The ref blows his whistle,
Everyone in position.

The team pull together,
In good or bad weather,
A goal is scored,
The crowd, they roared.

The win is ours,
We have used all our powers.

Football is the winner,
I'm off home for my dinner!

Jake Stanton (11)
Robert Bloomfield Middle School, Shefford

Family Symbols

Family is a word we all use
It is a symbol of unity
A symbol of love
A group of people to help when something is hard and tough.

Love is hard to describe
But wherever you go
Whether it's to see your grandparents, aunties or uncles,
There is always a surprise of love.

Unity is a little something we see every day;
It's like a community, where your family is here day by day.

Sometimes when you're feeling down
Just one smile from your family will sure to be found
If you're feeling sad, angry or even scared
Your family will be there all around.

Together and forever will your family stay,
Just remember to never change.

Basmah Malik (12)
Robert Bloomfield Middle School, Shefford

What Matters To Me

What matters to me
Is not what everyone can see
I care about books
But not my looks
That's what matters to me

What matters to me
Is not what everyone can see
Sleeping at night
Is a delight
That's what matters to me

What matters to me
Is not what everyone can see
My family is fun
I hate to run
That's what matters to me

What matters to me
Is not what everyone can see
School is a ball
My friends are tall
That's what matters to me.

Rachel Hookway (11)
Robert Bloomfield Middle School, Shefford

Herm Island

Herm Island is a place of joy
I've played there since I was a little boy
There is so much that you can do
There is so much for me and you
Lovely bluebells in the spring
And look what colours they all bring
Running through all the fields
Getting mud all up my heels
Jumping in all the sand
Smashing the water with my hand
Sound of laughter with my friend
A friendship that will never end
Throwing sticks, flying kites
Even climbing, huge, massive heights
Watching bunnies run free
And the sun on the sea
Camping's cool in a tent
All the pheasants know your scent
Playing leap frog with your friends
The fun just never, never ends
As we watch the sun go down
We count how long it takes to drown
Then we go to eat some tea
The food at the Mermaid is yummy
Herm is the greatest, it is my home
And always will be.

Toby Falla (15)
St Sampson's High School, Guernsey

What Matters To Me

The crystals falling from skies above,
Twirling round and round as they fall,
Their touch is gentle like a velvet glove,
They reach the ground without a single word.

The peaceful quietness of this world, only nature speaks,
The bare trees frosted with a single layer of snow,
Mountains covered up to the very peaks,
No animals, no humans, just me.

Roaring of a terrible creature gallops towards my ear,
They are dawning near, why should we let this planet suffer?
This land trembles with fear,
The world's nature matters to me.

Lucy O'Neill (12)
Tarporley High School, Tarporley

My Perfect House

If I had a house, my home would be,
Tall and smart just like me.
In each of the rooms you won't believe your luck,
From floor to ceiling it would be filled with books.
The swimming pool would be filled to the top with strawberry jelly,
Oh my God, look at the size of that telly!
My bed would be huge, fit for a king,
With gizmos and gadgets for everything.
Flashing lights and with gigantic bright colours.
Hmm, my bed is not unique; it's the same as my brother's.
My family would be there just as it is,
With healthy meals, security, big hugs and a kiss.
Anything could happen if I imagined it.

Jack Bennetts (11)
Tewkesbury School, Tewkesbury

What Matters To Me

The Earth we live on,
The clear blue sea.
The fresh green land,
That's what matters to me.

Every living species,
The blue whale to the bee.
Mysterious or deadly,
That's what matters to me.

My mum, dad and brother,
And the rest of my family.
Even my dog Zippy,
That's what matters to me.

All my dreams for the future,
A lawyer I want to be.
Fighting to keep that dream alive,
That's what matters to me.

Every wonderful memory,
Many a good one you see.
Encasing them forever inside my head,
That's what matters to me.

My irreplaceable friends,
Kind, crazy and happy.
All special and close to my heart,
That's what matters to me.

The life that I lead
Where I am totally free.
Free to choose my destiny,
And that is what matters to me.

Eleanor Gilbert (13)
Tewkesbury School, Tewkesbury

Friends And Family

F un to be around
R eliable but strange
I ncredible friends
E njoyable moments together
N ever let me down
D riving me forward
S o many memories that will last forever

F abulous relatives
A bsolutely great for giving advice
M agnificent and loving
I nspirational
L ooking out for me
Y ou and I can tell they are just great!

Verity Briggs (12)
Tewkesbury School, Tewkesbury

Come Together

Let peace be upon us,
Spreading throughout the Earth,
Let peace lift us,
Let it show what all of us are worth.

Let peace fill your empty life,
Every place and time,
Let peace free you of every strife,
Let us dispose of all war and crime.

Throughout the world there is war,
Hunger, famine - the world can't get any tougher,
And even though you give, try perhaps a little more,
If we work as one we can help those who suffer.

Kristina Bobs (12)
Tewkesbury School, Tewkesbury

My Family

My family have always been there for me
Helping me up and helping me see
The difference between right and wrong
When I'm with them I know where I belong

My family have always made me feel loved
Showed me things, like pigeons and doves
It's things like that that make me feel glad
And grateful for the life that I've had

My family have always showed me the way
Like a light in the darkness and a guide in the day
They told me if it's left or right
And to avoid that dog that bites

My family have always picked me up
When I've got grazed knees or bleeding cuts
They've cleaned me up and put me back on my feet
And told me again about playing in the street

My family love me for who I am
They don't care if I wear Donna Karan
They love me if I'm happy or sad
And I love them too because they're not that bad.

Emily Healey (13)
Tewkesbury School, Tewkesbury

Family

If I had to answer what's important to me,
I'd have to say it would be my family.
Whether it's a sister or a brother, or a father or a mother,
No matter what, they're always worth the bother.
They're always there to lend a hand
To help you out on first demand.
To cheer you up when you're down
To make sure you're left without a frown.
To kiss you better when you're ill,
To tuck you in when you feel a chill.
To answer your calls when you want to talk,
To hold your hand when you first start to walk.
To give you a hug when you're full of fear,
To brush away the last remaining tear.
To give advice when you've made a mistake,
To be the first face you see when you awake
And that's just the beginning for goodness sake

Ellie Hainsworth (13)
Tewkesbury School, Tewkesbury

Friends

Friends are those who are there for you when you are most in need.
Friends are those who care for you and do you a good deed.
Friends are those who support you in everything you do.
Friends are those who guide you and truly love you too.

Friends are those who make you cry.
Friends are those who tell you no lie.
Friends are those who make you glad.
Friends are those who won't make you sad.

Friends are those you treasure throughout your many years.
Friends are those who make you smile through your tears.
Friends are those who make you laugh and shout.
Friends are those you know you just can't live without.

Bethan Skuse (14)
Tewkesbury School, Tewkesbury

What Is Important To Me

Life is important to me
To be able to breathe the air
And leap through mid-air.
Be able to hit a hockey ball
And sing in the school hall.
Having a healthy beating heart
And a brain that is quite smart
Having friends I can trust
But not that I must
Being able to be led
All tucked up in bed
Because behind my four walls
There are no ghosts and ghouls.

Jenna Roberts (13)
Tewkesbury School, Tewkesbury

What Matters To Me

Family, friends
Are my first priorities
They make me smile, laugh and even cry
We have fun, chat and sometimes play
What they think matters to me
People poor and suffering living on streets
Make me feel sad and discreet
When they are happy I also am
People living in palaces make me feel glad
That they have somewhere
To live, happy and sad
If I had the opportunity
I would settle in mansions but if not receiving love I'd
Rather live on streets
This is what matters to me.

Enida Sadiku (11)
Walthamstow School For Girls, London

What Matters To Me

To me friends are really important
To have them you don't need any talent
True friends are those who can make you laugh
Sing and dance.

Naomi is always very cheerful
Even when I'm feeling awful
She puts a smile on my face
She is a friend that no one could ever replace.

Nicola is always so hyper
She's been my friend since forever
She always understands me when I tell her my troubles
And she often takes away all my problems

Maybe you're lonely and don't have anyone
But hiding away and being sad won't make you friends with everyone
So go up to someone and ask if you can play
They will surely say, 'Yay,'
After all, that's what friends are always for!

Amina Khanova (11)
Walthamstow School For Girls, London

My Goal

I like kicking the ball, so I can reach my goal,
I want to be a doctor and not just a proctor.
I want to be working very hard with strength and power even if it makes me sour.
I want to get good grades and work without being afraid,
And always doing my best to be better than the rest.
Where everything I'm learning is essential, I show my full potential.
I would go on and on improving tons on my academic elevation.
I have the ability to shine and design.
I will always increase but never decrease.
The ball is up high so I will touch the sky.

Samintha Thavarajah (11)
Walthamstow School For Girls, London

What Matters To Me

The world around
Everything
I see,
My lovely friends
And family.
The birds in
Their nests
The squirrels in
The tree,
That's what
Matters to me!

The buzzing bees
In their hive
The big brown fox
Stays up to jive.
The hedgehogs and
Prickly porcupines,
That's what matters to me!

All the people
That I see
My lovely friends
And family.
The teachers that
Taught me to
Read this poem to you.

My friends that
Taught me to
Have fun,
And all the cool
Things that
I've done.
It's such a joy
To be young,
That's what matters
To me.

But most of
All my family
The ones that
Mean so much
To me.
The ones I love
And adore the
Most, so wonderful
They are.
Sorry, got to go
That's the end
Of the show,
I hope you enjoyed
Finding out
What matters
To me!

Natalie Brady (11)
Walthamstow School For Girls, London

What Matters To Me

Having the thrill of my life
Watching scary movies
Eating chocolate and candy
All these things I very much adore
This may lead to a successful door

Sleeping and eating
Talking and listening
Reading and writing
All these things mean a lot to me
So I'll have to wait for what life has in store for me.

Something that matters
Something that's fun
Something I like
Something I want
All these things matter to me even though life is crazy
As we all have seen!

Namra Malik (12)
Walthamstow School For Girls, London

Education

Education is the key to success,
All children need it so their lives aren't a mess.
It is every child's right
Instead of doing labour in the night.
Very important is education
Should be available in every nation.
We all need to be learning
So that we can be earning.
Even if you're way too cool,
There's still means to go to school.
The entry to college
Is depending on your knowledge.
You need to be well educated
So you can have a job that's sophisticated.
Whether you're rich or poor
You need an education for sure.
We have to believe
As there's more to achieve!

Salma Patel (11)
Walthamstow School For Girls, London

What Matters To Me

What matters to me
Hmm, let's see.
Things that I like or want to be . . .
Or maybe more, but I can't be sure
So let's get on
Whether right or wrong.

The final score
A sound or melody
That smug little chuckle
When the rhyming's a felony!

That perfect smile
The smell of cut grass
That sigh of relief
When you finish a class.

Precisely plumped pillows
There for my head
When day turns to night
And I'm snug in my bed!

That unwritten poem
That swirls in my mind
When people do care,
When they are loving and kind.

That heart-warming fireplace
On a cold winter's evening
Holding cocoa in my hands
Thinking of Santa, truly believing.

A rousing speech
One of a kind
You've put loads of effort in
Care and time.

That magical touch
It's mine, not yours!
The sense of achievement
No mistakes, no flaws.

Revolutionising something
Making a stand
Democratic or civil
For poor, for grand.

All the things I have just said
Are all carefully placed in my head
My hopes, my dreams
The future, the past
All the things I have done so far!

My time's still to come
So please do not fret
This isn't the last
You ain't seen nothing yet!

Lola Grieve (11)
Walthamstow School For Girls, London

School

It's Friday morning 8.01
You're still half snoring, your homework's half done
Your shower is cold, your cornflakes are dry
Your mother forgets to slap you a goodbye

You're running to school, it's 40 degrees
You're burning to death, got coat on
You slip on school steps, you trip in class
The principal greets you by the wrong name
Your classroom is boiling hot, the coat rack is packed
Your maths partner's gone, your neighbour is rude
Your teacher's in a crabby mood.

The morning bell rings its 9.01
Oops, I'm late!

Atiya Pervez (11)
Walthamstow School For Girls, London

The Sweet Shop

Chocolate drops and creamy fudge,
Aniseed and minty sludge!
Curly lollies and liquorice wheels,
Sherbert lemons, some candy peels,
Fruit worms and strawberry dips,
Caramel wafts, I lick my lips.
Jelly babies, Tangtastics,
Gobstoppers, giant chewy sticks,
Pear drops and coconut ice,
Mint humbugs and sugar mice,
Gummy fruits and chewy toffee,
Mums and dads all drinking coffee,
Children watching, all stare
At the array that's waiting there!

Hannah Watkin (11)
Ysgol Gyfun Gymraeg Glantaf, Cardiff

Sweet Shop

My favourite shop is Yum Yum,
It's very far away.
In a place called Cardigan
Where I sometimes stay.

Yum Yum is a magical place
Full of sweets and treats.
Every time I go there
I don't know what to eat!

When I walk in through the door
The smell is just divine
Bonbons, sherbert, chocolate mice
All in the line.

I tell the lady what I want
'A bag of chew chews please,'
I give her fifty pence for them
And now they're all for me.

Nia Phillips (11)
Ysgol Gyfun Gymraeg Glantaf, Cardiff

Autumn

The cold wind blows
As the leaves rustle between my toes.

Red, yellow, orange are the leaves
Just waiting to fall from the high trees.

No warm sunshine or flowers
Only bare trees blowing for hours and hours.

Snow will soon come, so snowmen will make
While the mountains gaze over a frozen lake.

Tezni Bancroft-Plummer (11)
Ysgol Gyfun Gymraeg Glantaf, Cardiff

Sweets

Bubblegum and chocolate bars
Are all so munchy
I love them all so much
They are all so crunchy.

Liquorice and peppermints
Are my favourite treat
But I don't like butter scoops
They smell like smelly feet.

Rainbow stripes and sherbert
Oh dear, that's too sour
I'm having a painful
Toothache for hours.

So there's the different types of sweets,.
I'm going now to clean my teeth.

Amelia Smith (11)
Ysgol Gyfun Gymraeg Glantaf, Cardiff

Gobstoppers

A big, big thing that doesn't fit in my mouth
But deliciously tasty, a gobstopper.

Different colours and flavours all round
And deliciously tasty, a gobstopper.

Sucking and sucking all day long
And deliciously tasty, a gobstopper.

I've loved gobstoppers all my life
They're deliciously tasty, gobstoppers.

Mared Edwards (12)
Ysgol Gyfun Gymraeg Glantaf, Cardiff

Afghanistan

A love of a father and son,
The drone of a violent gun,
Bombs bursting all around,
I fly to the ground.

Shrapnel, metal, flying in the sky
The heart broken, my eyes cry,
Screams, shrieks, terror inside,
No longer a feeling of pride.

Dad, Dad, I cannot see
Dad, Dad, why aren't you with me?
Dad . . . Dad . . . please!
War - a dreadful disease.

Son, son, I love you still
Son, son, I do not want to read your will.
Son . . . son . . . I love you always
Even at the end of your days!

Llion Marc Carbis (11)
Ysgol Gyfun Gymraeg Glantaf, Cardiff

The Land Of Candy

Sugary, sticky, sickly treat
Which cause all kinds of perils beneath
Eat all you can until you feel rather ill
Till you're in a chair with terrible toothache
Oh sweets, you are highlights of our lives!

Emily Ogonovsky (11)
Ysgol Gyfun Gymraeg Glantaf, Cardiff

Waiting

Like King Canute I tried to halt
The tide of love which drowns my sorrow.
Alas! Aphrodite bears a fault!
A thousand hearts you could not borrow
To possess you, as I am possessed by thee.
Across four oceans I would swim,
To see the nymph that can answer my plea.
My belief flows from you, not Him,
It conquers my soul, floods my eyes.
Towards you a patriot, with you, a patriarch.

My love you can never chastise,
You can only return, so take me into your Ark,
You have the key to unlock my heart,
Turn it, remove the bolts constraining our lives,
Let our souls merge till death do us part,
Throw down your drawbridge, throw away your pavise
Cast the vile shackles and set us free,
Let our chords duet in harmony,
Or here, I shall forever be,
Waiting, waiting, upon one knee.

Sam Lipetz-Robic (17)
Ysgol Gyfun Gymraeg Glantaf, Cardiff

Golf

I started when I was six,
But needed little sticks.
Learning to hit the ball
So it landed in the hole.

Saturdays, when I was eight,
I was looking to hit it straight.
Sometimes in the rough
The next shot was very tough.

Tuesdays, when I was nine,
I practised all the time.
Hitting high and hitting low
In the rain and in the snow.

One day when I was eleven,
Playing the number seven.
I showed them how it's done
And had a hole in one.

I hope when I am older,
I'll have a giant folder.
Full of shots I have played
And all the putts I have made.

Rhodri Siôn Skyrme (11)
Ysgol Gyfun Gymraeg Glantaf, Cardiff

Gobstoppers

Giant gobstoppers,
In your small mouth for ages,
Sucking for so long.

So many sizes,
Small, big, giant and mega,
How would you suck them?

Sucking for so long,
Changing colour in your mouth,
What kind of colours?

Sizes and colours,
Loads of different gobstoppers,
Giant gobstoppers.

Caleb Roberts (11)
Ysgol Gyfun Gymraeg Glantaf, Cardiff

The Sweet Shop Magnet

As soon as the bell goes there's something I have to do
You are more than welcome to join me too.
It attracts you in if you walk straight past
When you get there you think at last!

The sweet and lollies all in a huge pile
The colourful walls and glittery tiles
The sweet smelling liquorice dangling from the sky
There's just no controlling us we just have to buy.

The sweets are so addictive and magical too
It's just like a drug there's no stopping you
All the flavours so magical and real
Three for a pound! What a great deal!

Holly McCormick (11)
Ysgol Gyfun Gymraeg Glantaf, Cardiff

Sweet Shop

I count my money
As it jingles in my pockets,
I enter the magic land
My eyes out of their sockets.

Jars of Heaven
Lie on the shelves,
Shivers of joy
Run through my blood cells.

Pear drops and bonbons
Of every size,
Liquorice Allsorts
And toffee surprise.

Turkish Delight
And fizzy lemons,
I think I've died
And gone to Heaven.

Just as I'm choosing
From the gazillions of sweets
My mum in the car
Gives a loud beep!

As I run out of Heaven
And back into Hell,
It's time for homework,
Oh well!

Elin Nia Lewis (11)
Ysgol Gyfun Gymraeg Glantaf, Cardiff

The Sweet Shop

I'm going to the sweet shop
To get some lovely treats
Shelves and shelves full of jars
The jars are full of sweets.

There are so many to choose from
Ooh! Which one? Which one?
Toffee, sherbert, Haribos
How about some bubblegum?

Well, the sweet shop owner
Is very kind indeed,
She always gives us discounts
And sweets for 50p.

We go there every Friday
After school obviously
Me and a bunch of friends
To spend our pocket money.

Hannah Roberts & Kirsty Louise French (11)
Ysgol Gyfun Gymraeg Glantaf, Cardiff

Sweet Shop

Hungry! Hungry!
Hungry for sweets!
Dad gave me money
For my favourite treats!

Gobstoppers, toffee,
Melt in the mouth
But the best one of all
Is the liquorice spout.

You suck the sherbert
On your tongue
But don't breath it in
'Cause it will go in your lung.

A bagful of sweets
In my hand
I forgot to pay
And now I am banned.

Mari Ann Bull (11)
Ysgol Gyfun Gymraeg Glantaf, Cardiff

My Dream Sweet

If I could create such a sweet,
That could kiss your tastebuds and tickle your feet,
I would sell it for money,
And serve it with honey,
And have it for a Saturday treat.

Once you've had one you'll always want more,
Whether you're rich or you're poor,
Alan Sugar would be proud,
And the guy in the cloud,
They will be knocking on my door.

That lad from the dentist will be on my back,
He'll say it'll make their teeth go black,
Although it's not very healthy,
It will make me very wealthy,
Who cares if their teeth are all covered in plaque?

Dafydd Manley (11)
Ysgol Gyfun Gymraeg Glantaf, Cardiff

Sweets And Teeth!

My teeth are important to me,
Bright and gleaming and filling free.
Liquorice, fudge, jelly beans and toffee,
Pear drops, sherbets and chocolate coffee,
Too many are bad for me, you see.

Take out a shilling and clasp it in my hand,
Scan the jars of humbugs and strawberry lace strands,
I lick my lips in satisfaction,
The shiny jars are my attraction,
Oh I love to visit the Sweet Shop Stand.

Sitting in the dentist chair,
I have a frightful scare.
Eating lots of sweets all week,
Are very bad for me to sneak.
Oh, I hate the dentist square.

Sioned Elin Rowlands (12)
Ysgol Gyfun Gymraeg Glantaf, Cardiff

If I Had The Choice

I would make real life sugar mice
In all flavours nice
Sherbet balls that when you suck
Fizz in your mouth and bring you good luck!

And chocolate snakes that wriggle and writhe
But don't let go as they'll slither and hide.
Toffee seeds soon to grow
Into toffee trees, you know.

Realistic sweetie pencils
That while you're sucking does your homework in seconds.
Chocolate eggs that over night
Hatch, and you have to catch as they all take flight.

When I go shopping
I want to see sweets popping.
Some fizzy, fizzy, fizzing
Others cracky-crack cracking.

Pink sweets that make you levitate
Ones that have the flavour of dinner on your plate.
Sweets that change colour in your mouth
That tingle pleasantly and make you laugh and shout.

Oh the things I would do, if I had the choice.

Molly Turner (11)
Ysgol Gyfun Gymraeg Glantaf, Cardiff

Fright Night

A fright night is coming,
A fright is in store,
For all the people in the world,
It's not Santa, it doesn't laugh joyfully,
It's not the Easter Bunny, it doesn't leave yummy treats.

If it gets you, your hair will turn white, your eyes will start popping out,
It will creep up on you at the dead of night,
It all starts as the sun goes down,
A vicious laugh at the dead of night.

If you hear laughter at the dead of night,
If you see a glow in the dark halls,
If you hear creaking floorboards,
If I were you, don't scream, or panic, it will sense it

But the big question is, what is it?
Is it a ghost, werewolf or worse?
Is it a . . . a, is it a . . .
Banshee with its screams?
A mad old woman will kill you
Her scream is too loud for human ears
They will bleed and you will die.

Ashbei Holland (13)
Ysgol Gyfun Gymraeg Glantaf, Cardiff

Sweets

Big, small, they make them all,
Everyone screaming for some more!
Hard, chewy, maybe even gooey,
Well, who cares, 'cause they're so yummy!

Sweet, sour, all covered in flour,
All the shops will be open for hours.
Sugar, juice, there's no excuse,
They're so tasty but also sickly.

Chocolate, sweets, such nice treats,
Nothing will stop us from eating both.
Tempting, tasty but don't be hasty,
Or you will get fat and you won't like that!

Morgan-Leigh McCarthy (11)
Ysgol Gyfun Gymraeg Glantaf, Cardiff

Feelings

Happiness is an ingredient
An ingredient of a heart
People smile when they're happy
People laugh when they're jolly but
You're the one who makes me happy.

So when you cry I know you're sad
A hundred tears makes me feel so bad and
Don't forget I will always be here for you.

Anger is an emotion you can't control
Nevertheless you should always let it go
Getting that feeling is like no other
Ready to explode your feelings to your mother
Yet you'll always feel better in the end.

Laughing and flirting with the boy you most adore
Only to find that he fancies the girl next door.
Very nasty that was of him
Every last hope was thrown in the bin.

Georgia Lewis (13)
Ysgol Gyfun Gymraeg Glantaf, Cardiff

Young Writers Information

We hope you have enjoyed reading this book - and that you will continue to enjoy it in the coming years.

If you like reading and writing poetry drop us a line, or give us a call, and we'll send you a free information pack.

Alternatively if you would like to order further copies of this book or any of our other titles, then please give us a call or log onto our website at www.youngwriters.co.uk

Young Writers Information
Remus House
Coltsfoot Drive
Peterborough
PE2 9BF
(01733) 890066